Chinese Apples

Chinese Apples

NEW AND SELECTED POEMS

W. S. Di Piero

ALFRED A. KNOPF · NEW YORK · 2009

THIS IS A BORZOI BOOK
PUBLISHED BY ALFRED A. KNOPF

www.aaknopf.com

Knopf, Borzoi Books, and the colophon are
registered trademarks of Random House, Inc.

A list of previously published poems appears on page 247.

Library of Congress Cataloguing-in-Publication Data
Di Piero, W. S.
Chinese apples : new and selected poems / W. S. Di Piero.—1st ed.
p.   cm.
ISBN: 978-0-375-71143-5
I. Title.
PS3554.I65C47 2007
811'.54—dc22   2006047383

Published February 8, 2007
First Paperback Edition July 15, 2009

149137329

This book is for Daniela
in good faith

CONTENTS

FROM *The Dog Star* (1990)

_____

FROM *Skirts and Slacks* (2001)

FROM ***Brother Fire*** (2004)

New Poems

FROM

The Only Dangerous Thing

(1984)

Four Brothers

1.

Pino the lizard in his patent leather shoes
wears cologne none of us ever heard of,
though he's told us at least a dozen times,
Pinaud, you dopes. It's French. Who cares?
All we know is hearsay, and what we see
depends on what we know. Pino's the one
who made it big, the only brother of three.
There would have been a fourth, but for something
Mrs. Pino did one night to the last born
because she felt too old or tired. Nobody
talks about it. That was years ago. Now Pino
works outdoors, selling nickel bags to blacks,
writing numbers, lending money to men
outside the neighborhood. He doesn't know
how short his life will be, that one fine day
he'll blink and won't be there to see himself
the way we see ourselves in how we act.
The first time men in good suits came
to take him to jail, one big honest afternoon,
we stood outside and watched Mrs. Pino
stiff in her doorway, silent, while the car door closed
as if a stranger's hand had pressed a pillow
on an infant's face, then held it there.

2.

Out of respect, or danger, nobody talks
about the oldest, Frankie, as if he were
religion. I don't understand his story,
which loiters in its mystery as stories do.
The morning after the youngest died, Frank
locked himself inside his upstairs room.
He's lived there ever since. His mother leaves
sandwiches, papers, cigarettes,
while Frankie listens to the radio
and draws those movie faces, all big names,
Carole Lombard, Rita Hayworth, Marilyn,
sending sketches out with half-eaten meals.
Gifts to his mother, I think, some revenge,
to punish her with images of ladies
who love wild light, real stars who don't
have to remember anything. Frankie
isn't crazy, but he needs certain things.
I catch myself waiting for him to die,
as if I knew he'd leave me charcoal sticks
or pads or a picture of himself. The worst
would be to find he left nothing, cared nothing
about remembering or being remembered.
He must need memory to make his art.

3.

Sally may be trucking through pine barrens
or selling taffy to Camden Puerto Ricans.
Hating both his brothers, snorting what's left of love
while he drinks with the Strongman in Toms River
or buys thread with the Blockhead in Wilmington.
He watched Frankie go upstairs, saw skinny Pino
driven off to prison, and he knew even more.
So he joined the carnival. I saw the ad:
SEE STRANGE SALVATORE EAT WILD FIRE!
I try to see the strange places he must love
passing through, his mouth his only real house,
each night those knots of fire, big fists between
his lips, past his teeth, down the tunnel to his belly,
all fire in the center of him, then save it all
at the final second. *Pull out the fire! Pull it out!*
Later, closing the show in mud and fog, he hauls
canvas with a midget and runaway murderer.
We all know that the carnival brings rain.
Sally must know everything and not need
memory, only his mouth in a pillow,
breath trapped in fire deep inside his throat
while he sleeps with two women, or a man,
owing himself only the need to go and go.

Jewana Got Gypped

He's got rubies and emeralds stashed
somewhere in his cellar. Saturday nights,
he cruises Camden's strip joints. Frilled shirt,
sapphire cuff links, jazzbow, old crow's voice—
My name's Giuana, what's yours? You like me?
See these cuff links? You like them? I give them to you!

He comes down Watkins Street, Thursdays, at dusk,
the orange sky smearing through telephone wires.
Supper smells leak from houses. We sit
on Crazy Charlie's steps, making a torch
with broom handle, rags, and glue
for a midnight run on Halloween.

Then Jewana, feet wrapped in leather flaps tied
with greasy string, pushing a Penn Fruit cart
top-loaded with mismatched sneakers, wire,
collapsed Wheaties boxes and a plastic cutlass.
We go hollering after him in the almost dark,
Jewana got gypped! Jewana got gypped!

He hates us more than we hate ourselves. *Ma va, stronzini!*
I'll punch you little fucker faces and fry your balls for breakfast.
Then you'll see who got gypped! We like him,
but we're afraid of his craziness. He's not us.
When he's mad his neck turns to raw meat
and his jaw is a coyote. He's not us.

Once somebody threw a brick that nicked him
and knocked him down. We didn't think he'd die,

but I saw a bloody thread slide down his ear,
it stopped at the corner of his jaw, then dripped off.
I hated him then, hated his bleeding, his rich blood.
He swore back at us, at his blood. *This is you.*

He ignored my life. I hated him for that. He's not me.
Go see the coal bin he lives in, Yom-Yom told me. *I swear
there's diamonds all over the place.*

I saw them.

Diamonds.

Aurelio

When I see mules lurching down the hillside,
tobacco sheaves quivering like rag mops,
I can't see myself anywhere else.
My village is a failing hive,
the young swarming into adulthood
to feed the honeycomb America. Wives
alone by their doors, watching the dust;
daughters in pairs buying bread and salt.
They clutch their purses as if the world lived there.
Nobody asks why so many men are old.

There's real work on the other side, the old new world,
nobody's promised land, just a place to work
for real. Sometimes need is a plague—we don't know
who died first, only that hundreds are dying now.
The good life, a rumor, a hidden mossy well,
nice shoes, new friends, streetcars, good cigarettes,
I trust this bountiful hearsay only when
I'm not here, planted like one more tree
on this hard bare hill, but better dust than lies
and stupid dreams, yet I dream of the sea:

I'm on my hilltop in Abruzzo. Dwarf pines, fennel,
a spill of vines halfway down. The distant sea
solid hard golden blue. On the shore,
children gather wood to feed a bonfire.
Chairs, schoolbooks, pencils, the moon high and bright.
As the fire blooms, they undress one another
and fondle like lovers, small bodies in yellow shade
fused to firelight and sand, then disappear.

I wake, smoke a cigarette by my window
where dung carts are creaking by in twilight.

My wife and young son know me in passing.
I'll leave them to prepare to meet them.
It's all right if I eat silence, cool green
olive leaves flashing dark on my skin,
and it spills from me into my boy and he
will pass it on to his sons to come
in a mess of cities. Marriage bed to steerage bunks
and blankets, when she'll be an invisible vineyard
just beyond my reach, across water. I imagine
later she will come to join me, the baby

grabbing at ocean spray because he sees me there,
to grow up with a new language in his mouth
and a choice of names to invent his life.
I see him as a young man, hollow-cheeked
like me, a brown photograph, posed with cigarette,
an alert hungry wolf self-contained
among strange brickface, a tangle of briar
in his blood. He thinks of his dead father
who crossed the sea, who is silent in
the future because what's to come is now.

Vincenzo Tailor

Say Vincenzo, an ordinary name, nicer than my last,
which I don't think I remember anymore,
maybe because a lady I met in Tangier
called me Ahmad Muhammed and wanted me,
so after five days' shore leave I believed
my name was Ahmad. What difference does it make
to you? In Málaga a lady called me Domingo,
like a guitar string, so I was Sunday for a week,
and I loved that woman though I think
she stole my wallet the day I said goodbye.

New York City is like history in tar, a pit,
and I could have been in Australia for all I knew,
drunk three days on the docks, so I invented
myself Irish—O'Brian, I think, or Kavanaugh.
A name should be what you do, and what you do
should grow in your soul like hair on your head.
So say Vincenzo, which is true, and Tailor because
that's what I was before shipping out with okra,
transistor radios, wheat, slippers, cheese, boots,
coffee beans, pistols, typewriters, handkerchiefs . . .

That was thirty years ago. Now my brain forgets,
but my hand remembers the feel of needle and thread.
Yesterday I had to sew my shoe. My hands are still good.
I wasn't like this. I didn't sit in Horn & Hardart's
asking a stranger to buy me coffee. These times
are temporary. They'll go. I'll stay. Coffee's good
with chicory. In Naples people knew
a suit I made would last forever. Like magic.

But I needed money, so I went to sea.
Whoever said the sea would make me rich?

Shanghai, Lisbon, Liverpool, Valparaiso,
I've seen all these places. I appreciate a stranger
who buys me coffee. You know who I am?
If you want a suit I'll make it for you. Go to
the Seaman's Lodge on Chestnut Street, ask for Vincenzo,
or Vincent, or Vinnie—those old guys there,
they'll know who you mean. I never forget a stranger.
See this button? Oyster shell I carved in Rio,
and this bracelet I wove from baling wire in Cefalù.
I like the sound of water here. Schuylkill. Delaware.

Saxophone

Sunlight slams off car windows
and belts the sawdust floor.
The surfaces of Sunday morning.
Peanut bowls, ashtrays, crinkled
cigarette packs, shuffleboard pucks,
the cupped upturned hands of men
standing at the club bar,
members only, and their sons,
a local place for locals.
The set goes on all morning.

Georgie takes me in his lap,
shows me how to stretch my fingers,
to reach for husky changes until
the webbing feels about to split
and I worry who will heal me.
My small hands want the lacquered
brassy promise of power locked
down there. Power to hold sound back,
a music unfound inside, made real
once it goes unstopped, unsealed.

I touch a spiny key, the scene changes:
warped butcher block, me standing there,
list wilting in my fist, chicken cages rattling,
the acidic stink of feathers, dung, offal,
a dozen dialects in beak and mouth,
the butcher shouting at Italian women
who talk about the old country, hunger,
oxblood cooled to gelatin, carob chocolate.

And Negro ladies wanting pig ears, oxtails,
telling of Alabama whipsnakes that coil

around your leg and beat you to death as you run.
The butcher's blade glistens through
bright flesh. The women watch him slice,
then look out the windows the way music looks
away from itself, while my hands fall asleep
on Georgie's, the sax's sound swaddling me
in solace softer than time and space,
more than the here and now where dark men
chase shots with beer, laughing hard
into a weariness of days and nights.

I'm jazzing one day and picture to the next,
past checker players smoking stogies,
tough boys in tight pants, hard-toned black girls
in flats and fleecy blouses, shop fronts
bright with bikes, tiles, cribs, and drill bits,
while across them afternoon shadows fall,
all loud and plentiful as Georgie's sound,
pumping and huffing in my guts like speech,
toward some misted life not yet my own
where I'll become the music I have been.

Smoke

We loiter in the cobblestone alley,
Beans, Clams, Yom-Yom and me,
smoking punk. Snip the wiry stem,
trim the nubby end, scratch fire
from a zipper then pass the stink around.
William Penn designed these blocks
squared off, brick, crosshatched by alleys
to prevent the spread of fire. So fire
runs down my throat, reed
turning to iron inside my lungs.

Yom-Yom has an uncle in Bucks County.
Country boys sneak behind barns and puff
on cedar bark. Smoke's the only thing
we have in common. Smoke when our breath
meets cold moist air, though no smoke rings
in winter, while sullen cars drag gray on gray
down city streets or country roads.
Someday I'll smoke Camels, my father's brand,
then Gauloises to prove I'm stronger than him
in burning whatever's inside that won't sleep.

Strates Shows

Under oblong bellies raked by dirt and moonlight,
past big-toothed tires, fat axles bleeding grease,
the holy circle of twenty diesel semis,
on my hands and knees through mule chips, straw,
cigar butts, gum wrappers, candy-apple nubbins,
emerging just off the midway. JEDEDIAH
THE HUMAN BLOCKHEAD *and* EX–RHODES SCHOLAR
See him drive 6-inch STEEL SPIKES *and* RAZORTIPPED AWLS
into his HUMAN *skull.*
                              The loony bins flicker
red and yellow beside the rolling Ferris wheel:
Herman the Strong *Bends Iron Bars.* Pretty Boy Floyd
with lipstick, violet eyelids, straw hair to his hips.
When he bats his lashes, I can't look away,
as if this was my first time, yet I keep coming back
until the known gets even stranger. I feel
I'm always just arriving, out from under trucks.
A schooner squirms on Olaf's tattooed pecs:
its inky hold bears jars of quince from China,
Romanian goose down plucked by gypsy hands,
years of hiding in smoky camps on plains.
The roustabouts are gypsies of some kind.
Carnival is when you're not what others make you.
I tell myself there's nothing more to them
than what I see—stitched surfaces, the buffed face
of the real in the absence of stories. Then
I remember those jars of quince, those gypsy hands,
the fuzzy eye of Madame Simba's crystal ball:
"You shall live only long enough until
you stop. Become. Become. Others don't

make up the world, they help you to invent it."
Bearish shadows crash across the scuffed tent.
Light hurts Madame's eyes. "Eat what you can't see,
what you need to know is there. I predict
you will feel guilty for seeing too much.
Will sleep be a friend? You want real joy?"

FROM

Early Light

(1985)

Canada

The half-dark of morning,
maples rash with fall's
early burning, and north,
beyond the solemn tree line,
the stifled bark swelling
until it broke clean free:
the air split and crackled
and a swoon of Canada geese
widened above against
the gray unstirred heights.

You ran, still in your robe:
from its sailing blue skirts
to the tiny gold crosses
on your ears, you burst
off the porch, across
the grass, pitching your breath
toward the seasonal flight,
to see them just that once,
once hear annunciation
in the passing trace.

The Call

They sit and talk two rooms away,
mother and daughter in the morning.
I don't know what they say, maybe
a silly tale of a girl who dreams
her way to a tree: a dragon lives
inside, and other rooms stacked below
lead to a secret pool and stream.
But I don't hear this, only
the woman's mannish hum pierced
by the child's blissful whispers.
I remember this on top of something else:
my parents grumbling in their room,
words sucked down into the swamp.
They, too, uneven lengths of sound
chopped by doubts, pauses, upliftings.
And Orpheus couldn't have known
it wasn't that bright girl's voice
that called him. All he knew, bounded
by the mineral set of a world
unchanged below, was his compulsion
to turn. Maybe he paused and argued
with himself: to what shade or room
would his lover go? What blood-seamed rock
welcome, then return, her vague speech,
and to whom? And thought of what
she may have meant to tell him while
they climbed, keeping that space between:
We will listen to the worst
and wait, wanting more, because
of what we think we need to know.

You never loved me so much
as you loved voices from the dark.
Pitch and burr mattered more
than any touch or sight.
For this I loved you, in my way.
For this you will not know me.

A Greater Good

An autumn morning,
slabs of yellowflake light
canting through the pines.
Files of crisp boys and girls
walk hand in hand, pressed
by planes of air. Their bright
eyes see everything except
whatever lies ahead,
promise such a lesser thing.
What final place makes claims
on their desire? They go
without knowing the day,
week, or hour, traveling
absolute in a commonwealth
of mist and pinned shade.
Brilliantine flash of shoes,
vinyl bookbags, painted buttons.
No greater good for them
beyond the skittish talk
of a leafstorm at their feet.

To Suffice

Prayer merely happens,
a visit, unquestioned,
a power outside the house
that suddenly fills each room.
It happens in the morning,
usually in fall, when the light
booms with other seasons,
a green ground for spring
masked by summer's bluegold
haze, with winter's powdered
ores spread all around
as huge confining promise.

I don't go on my knees
or look up toward that other,
but wait, in silence, until
table, cup, and spoon become
burdened fortunately with light.
It takes from me everything
I never knew I had,
and gives more than enough
of that which has no use,
a bounty announced inside,
figure ground of sun on pond,
the heavens on the floor.

On Mt. Philo in November

Dawn again and
the wind is harvesting
weed trees—aspen, birch.
Plum light wrinkles
puckerbrush
where deer slept.
A spider clings
to a blade of grass
then climbs down
a maple leaf.
The wind lifts
and tumbles them past.
All things living
on nerve alone.
Autumn's instinct
to travel, a tedium
dropped and blown
toward ice and snow-ledge.
Soon lumps of frost
will bend branches
and my hands will
burn on touch.
Winter will be
the effort to live.
Autumn now
is the compulsion
to get that far.

Gold

The father, for no reason, lifts his rake
to heaven, while his children form
a broken ring around him. The girl
sits on a pile of leaves, snapping stems.
The boy looks to his father's hands
raised high to hold the hour.

A mess of wind above arrests them
in their work: the broad maple
bows hard once, back and forth,
and shakes down its leaves like summer's
shooting lights, a gashed mineral
storm, an earnest from the sky.

In the bell of streaming embers,
in the collapse and casting off,
father, girl, and boy are gathered,
dissolved, and they become another
time, another bunched fire bonded
by particularities of light.

Lucky Lucy's Daily Dream Book

Provision for the day? Gloss
on what stopped by in sleep?
Sweet categories, gypsy
oracles, three numbers
you can bet on, mysteries
that explain your common ways:

A running horse runs lucky
(no matter lack of wealth)
in marriage; but if he falls
in flaming pools, death comes
drumming on the window.
Believe in God. Take care.

There was also, somewhere,
a moss-stained church
blocking the way (it says here)
to new sexual delight.
Wait a while. The stones
may turn to gold and fall.

A sailor skipping on deck
means news, good clothes,
certain weather for prospects.
If it rains on him, beware
your children's love, the bruise
of chance, and formlessness.

To dream a garden never known
where mica grows with peppers,

that's tomorrow. That's the gift
of small mortality. Tend it,
pray, embrace its promise
of short gorgeous nights.

The Husband's Song

The details she calls normal worries
soften her in the morning. There
in her nightgown, by the stove,
fooling with jets and pans,
blank face and shoulders still
puffed and pulled by sleep,
she works to settle into time
dawn lets loose.

                 "Did you dream much?
Maybe I shouldn't ask
what you've seen."

                 "Our daughter,
kidnapped years ago by you. A sister
I never had who betrayed me somehow.
A smiling friend who brought me pearls,
black pearls that became corn on fire
in my hands."

                 Not to let these go
until they make some kind of sense,
until these first chores are done,
her fingers drift too close
to the flame, breaking in between,
that keeps us not unhappily apart.

Turning

I don't know how to unsay the cry that breaks
behind the door. My sleeping daughter runs
through birches and wants, I suppose,
a good thing—gaudy doll or butterfly—
something new and out of reach. I imagine
she sees, in the light-cracked door,
one who will someday come to revise
her plain-faced certainties and ruin,
more than once, what she hopes most from love.

She'll turn in another bed and look past
starlight's nest to the moon, a shell
her lover gave her, glossed by time,
in which she heard the sea strain one day
on the beach, his hand on hers, sweat
across her brow. From that sunlight she'll turn
to face the moon and its divisions,
the sullen mediating glow I now see falling
through the window on her shut eyes.

The Incineration: Kansas

The elevators, a hundred miles away,
wrinkling on a watery band of dawn,
the bread of other seasons stored there
out of reach, unstuck from the horizon . . .
The prairie rises toward that land's-end line,
then goes beyond, where we may never see.

———————

Flourishing from last season's stubble,
juncos belly up and heave toward us
and vanish in the light behind and
switching back, reel and are embodied
once again, as if the Grace who returns
her gifts could not be caught or guessed.

———————

Next morning, laying the Christmas wraps
and ribbons on the rusted oil-drum's fires,
we watch each other across the broken smoke,
the reds and greens go down while ashes
drift back up, dusting the new sun, faces
configuring in the air what's near and going.

December 28: Returning to Chicago

Let's assume the stars
dropped, undiminished
in our sight, then cooled,
beading on the new snow.
From our train we see
the sulfur pips of houses
at enormous distances,
the land extending
like a thought that's fine
only when it dares
its own expanse. Headlights
carve that emptiness.

Back home, the lights go up,
not away (stacked floor
by floor, ledge by ledge,
the living sites, tools,
duties, songs tried, tiered,
decked and balanced)
waiting for the new year
to exalt or dim them.

Easter Service

He half expects a Chinese dragonhead
will bloom from the weave of golden chasuble,
its fangs grinning behind some scalloped fire.
Choir voices surround the lifted chalice,
the elemental dying God wrapped
in music made to storm the sky and purge
the debris of fact. He vaguely sings along.
To his ear it seems a belated howl,
or rude oversimplified foretelling.

Outside the big dome, the rain keeps falling
on shrubs still curtailed, stumped by the slashed
cold air. The unseasonal chill determines
spring's delay; green stuff on its own knows
what to do. The windows, too, are changed.
St. John keeps his shape but the colors cross,
pressing green on red. The lamb's fleece
gleams darkly, the backlight's too unsteady.
The voices run like color down the walls.

On such a morning, he stood on deck and watched
the sullen Azores, not at heaven's distance,
taking the sun while he sailed past. Or:
he held still, the landmass drifted by,
unshadowed, absorbed by such deep brilliance,
as if its body was never actually placed
or brought into the light. Certainly no thought
of God, but maybe earth's rank intelligence,
another holiness, heavy flowers of the sea.

He was the privileged witness, and messenger
to himself, mind to mind, earth's thought thinking.
But if he passed again he'd surely see
a different phase of dark, the littoral shaved
and notched by waves. The new Atlantic swell
would lift him toward the land he thought he knew:
the vegetal islands, flexed in memory,
have become anxious hungry animals,
their voluptuous distance lived in, never crossed.

Newfound robins, redbirds, branches rough
with leaf buds, hedgerows still disclosing
their entanglements, church-organ wail
muted by stone while the sky soon goes
from gray to stunned oceanic green.
But here at Mass there is no history.
The core translation, human and divine,
repeats a million times, each time true,
a fixed thickened everlastingness.

Simpleminded, expectant, a little aroused
by what she's learned, the reverent Mary comes
to find a gorgeous boy slouched by the tomb,
his voice a skein of wind and water. Offhand,
he says that He has risen. Her confusion
worsens with belief. Spread the news.
Tell the others that stone-bound earth,
its molten core, couldn't hold the man God.
Tell them they will never die again.

Incense drenches the air, a smoky figure
of praise designing the high old trace,
then gone. Then more, again. He tells himself
he cannot die, and his insistent hoot,
aggrieved angel-noise, reminds him that belief
isn't knowledge. Desire becomes unfleshed,
intelligence a fulsome ghost, or dream,
and he feels the gravity of life lift
in music's praiseful vaporous dance.

But there was also unnerved January.
The sun at 7 a.m., a dragonhead
above the lake, an ungrieved liquid sun
smarting the lakeside snowdump mounds that smoked
as if the seasonal thaw had really come.
The new light scorched the icebound fields
and picked up millions of silvered points
washing down the street to meet him. Or not meet him.
He walked east anyway, to enter that place,

as if creation, while it comes undone,
could tell him what was there beyond all this.
Unrecorded stars, the happy chaos cry
of galaxies, other voices he might hear
and yet not understand. That's what he knows
of heaven. And all. That's the angry crossing
to the mind outside his own. It's what he hears
in the infinite covered space stuffed with song
that curves, unsettled, inside his desperate ear.

Fat Tuesday

I'll lick these screwfaced torches all night long
and chew the beads and blue doubloons sailing
from iron balconies mossy in the dark.
I'll walk down Royal Street dressed as a sweet-gum,
pretending my back is front, whiskey-breath for all
who love a season of pretending. I'm ready
for denial, to put away sweet fat things and spoils,
the meat and heavy jewels of wanting
anything, even the wish to want.
The King salutes us from his golden dragon.
He's our food today. Eat his bones, his furs,
his crown and scepter. Eat his fat throne and flesh,
his voice that laughs us into easy forgiveness.
I'll eat the King and break his will inside me
and toward tomorrow mix him with these swallowed
pearls and coins and whiskey and days.

In Preparation

In a summer's hurricane field
the air slurs with the plump,
oily nearness of windstorm rain.
Before it breaks, I count the buds
and barkribs rolled up in the air,
each a thing apart, all lumped whole.
Storm perfect in its promise,
a futureness in color, volume:
seaweed crape myrtle trunk,
liveoak leaf pulled down toward
a big-thighed root, camellia rot
soaking the ground under me.
The world puffs and shines.
And comes here, new, exact,
before it finally comes for real.

In Our Room

On the strip between the lakes
I look for some trace of you
in everything that moves.
At the tip of its wake, a coot's
bone bill points through
the leaves' sponged-ink shade,
slate feathers splitting the air;
the water quivers, bright
as your bath-drenched hair
shaking off silvered bits.
A tern pulls up, tilting
through the spreading light,
then drops beak and body fast.
Two dark swifts dip past
swamp oaks like brown
twilight in our room, blinds
barring your face, while your lips
closed on some dream sound,
some word I didn't catch,
a wood-duck's straight-seamed wedge,
a cowbird shuddering from
the lake on loose bent wings.

Two Poems in Spring

1.

One day, when nothing important happened,
in South Philadelphia's St. Edmond's Church
a woman on the last night of novena
looked at the altar and said to the small
scarlet flame hanging from gold chains
that her descent had started—preparations
complete, the children gone, her sister
claiming chunks of raw meat in the kitchen—
and that heaven was queen to all, she said,
and the crude light staining her fingers
was water of plenty that she would drink down
to the bones in her unnecessary hand.

2.

Too much at once when I was a boy and stood
by my bedroom window. In the square shadows
thrown by roofs and cinder-block fence,
I saw two giants wrestling. Their moves
called up a sudden garden where they fought—
persimmon trees, and almond blossoms blowing,
fleshy azaleas lunging after pansies,
a flash of brassy lemon leaf tucked
in their big elbows. Then sounds assembled:
tires on rain, cop cars yelling, leaves,
some dialect jangle next door, sneakers
hung from telephone wires thumping
in the wind that shot the alley and blew
those arm-locked giants into my smallish room.

Early Light

The wooden blinds, opening,
take and measure the luxurious
trace cast by stars and moon,
a falling I think to follow
back to its distant source,
knowing that what comes near
too often touches me because
it's withheld, out of reach
in sight. The light mocks versions
of desire. The blinds don't stir.

One Sunday morning, years ago,
I watched churchgoers gather
inside the onion dome's shade:
Russians were stranger than
anything I knew—a choked
speech, wolfhide, sunlit nights,
fugitives from snowy wastes,
their Christ a gilded anguish.
Yet they had come to pray.
I stood outside, waiting,
while they entered and began
to sing. Fused words swarmed
into pillared voices lifted
through roof and dome
to that parting of the sky
where winter light spilled down.

Songlight, lightsong, one
element of air bonded of

what broke as terrible
rejoicing. And I sang, too,
but it was more shout
than song, more a wish
to be what that song was.
Indifferent constellations
are instantly beautiful,
solar light breaks against
lunar dark, an instant's
worth no more than any sign
arriving brilliantly
too late. And I think it all
a gift, blind grace, or blessing
on the child's needful cry.

But it's not true. What seems
to come from nowhere lies.
Or I lie for its sake.
Prayer becomes oblivion.
The stars outside my window
explode out into themselves
to deliver early light.
Moon, stars, soon day breaking,
the grave dream dreamed elsewhere,
never, I know now, for me.

FROM

The Dog Star

(1990)

The Ice Man

Like toads they've never seen,
squat behind graystone
steps, or knotted in alleys,
the children watch themselves
disappear from his sight.

He exists only in the hour
of the gift, in the black
open-hatched truck housing
their desire. They wait
until he walks away,

watching the forms inside,
blocks shaved and milky,
winter's air tensed and saved
for August, with something
stellar at the center,

an aurora or shattered core,
December's anger splintered
in frozen puddles bursting
underfoot, mouths
grinning up at them.

In a mountaintop town
in the impossible Andes,
parents tell their children
that all song once began
chanted by the Milky Way,

but mysteriously froze
into the ragged trail
summer heat someday
would thaw and heaven's sound
will shower on our heads.

When he finally walks away,
the vague blockhead solemn
on his shoulder, they leap
into the box and steal
pieces of dogstar days.

Lunar needles, hatchet-
heads, sea horses,
the air outside still gummed
with tar fumes, roofs
not yet cooked and poured.

Eating ice, ice,
atonement's song, boots
breaking new snow—
so easy to walk away
from the fear of being found.

How can they know
the unseen ice man traps
and loves them for their nerve?
That his bright remains
always wait for them?

The Adoration

The black stargazer
lurches closest
to the manger, his hand

stabbing deep shadow
between the rough nest
and his gift:

a golden urn
balanced like fruit
on his open palm.

At his heels in December's
feeble snowfall,
the cheerless, paleface magus

cringes as if he's glimpsed
unwanted and too soon
his own rich man's image

in the wet church stones
bulking behind the stable.
He holds no gift.

Ignored by the donkey, lambs,
rooster and camel
on the famished hallowed lawn,

their plastic skins
swell and glow
as the dark intensifies

the puffy light within
that would explode them
where they stand.

The angry third studies
heaven through the grid
of red and green bulbs

canopied overhead
like a carnival or car lot,
bleeding out the starlight

that fades before it reaches
the off-center crib,
where the Child, grinning

and inattentive,
watches His balled fist
push back at the night sky.

Walt, the Wounded

The whole world was there, plucking their linen,
bald, mumbling, sucking on their moustache tips,
Broadway was still in business and they asked no favors.

All the cracked ribs of Fredericksburg,
the boys who held their tongues at Chancellorsville
as the bandages, mule shit, skin and shot

overran the Rappahannock's banks
and poured it in their mouths
that summer.

He sat up half the night reading to the Army of the Potomac
poems about trooping goats and crazed fathers
chewing grass in the wilderness.

> *It's me that saved his life, dear mother.*
>
> *He had dysentery, bronchitis, and something else*
> *the doctors couldn't properly diagnose.*
> *He's no different than the others.*
>
> *I bring them letter paper,*
> *envelopes, oranges, tobacco, jellies,*
> *arrowroot, gingersnaps, and shinplasters.*
>
> *Last night I was lucky enough*
> *to have ice cream for them all*
> *and they love me each and every one.*

The early teachers stretched on canvas cots
with their bad grammar, backs smeared by pounders,
arms and legs heaped underneath a tree

about a load for a one-horse cart. At night,
campfires peaked by shebangs in the bush.
He'd find the stage-drivers laid up there—

Broadway Joe, George Storms, Pop Rice, Handly Fish,
Old Elephant and his brother Young Elephant (who came later),
Yellow Joe, Julep Tarn, Tick Finn, and Patsy Dee—

the pinched khaki drifting down gangways,
home-comers looking for those not waiting there,
bamboo lays and punji sticks in their dreams.

A small fire burns in the nursery.
Rice and molasses simmer on the stove.
Children will have to learn to ask for less,

less from the elephant dawn that chilled
across the heights where Lee held his ground.
The sky curled its wrath around the land

and they brought America's fire home.
Fire on our hands, ashes at Bull Run, buckets from Pleiku,
while he stood watching on the shore, pulling his beard.

America seems to me now, though only
in her youth, but brought already here,
feeble, bandaged, and bloody in hospital.

Our roughed-up beauties dead or dying,
he sang them goodnight with hands in his pockets
who would have kissed them and warmed their flesh.

When Oscar F. Wilbur asked if he enjoyed religion:
Perhaps not, my dear, in the way you mean,
and yet may-be it is the same thing.

To worship the fire in the nursery, fire in cities
and deserts, among those we love, to worship
what burns because we cannot help ourselves.

The Bugler

The sound's ribbon curves
over the heads of mourners
choired around blooms,
purple sashes, folding chairs,

crimped and foiled
in high winds that rock
the boy's marbled shako.
Listing, heels locked,

he's prepared to chase
each lacquered tone, stop it
at the brightening point
where sky soaks it up.

Or call brayed song back,
suck it in, graveside,
so he can make grief small
once it's safe inside.

May Queen

While parents in the crowd
crane their necks to follow
the long white trail that bends
around the church corner
out of sight, not
of our imagining,

your pace, vulnerable girl,
measures every prayer,
hands pressed to an arrow,
head bent over your beads,
lace tiara nodding tall
and feathery in Maytime air

like a single fern, in a house
now dark, suddenly fixed
in its singleness by lights
switched on when all come home,
yet stirring vaguely, untouched
by any sweet wind,

or like (against all reason)
the warrior's horsehair crest
clawing from his helmet down
toward his child, who starts,
cries out at the unnamed
monster from the sky,

and no soothing words
from mother or attendant

can quiet the baby who sees
a father dressed in blood, dirt–
battered, his face dust-drawn,
stranger to every kindness.

Second Horn

(Venice, 1975: Scuola di San Giorgio degli Schiavoni)

The sparks showering off the paint
kindle in her gray head—on the wall,
fierce and concentrated, St. George
pushes the lance until it shatters
in the scrawny teeth. Her hand goes up to hold
the point erupting behind the roaring skull:
the dragon's second horn, a warrior's gift
to nature. To kill exaggerated life
is surely goodness, the world's design
shouldn't be smeared. There's no good reason.

A crooked sense in her bones,
she walks the tangled shade of wash lines
and antennas. In the café, with friends,
she tells again what they've heard a hundred times
and she as often forgets.
That once, in Rome, she saw the Duce,
close as that chair, and if she'd had a gun
she would have shot him, because in him she saw
that German Devil, God's worst part,
O kill the Devil where you find him!

The others listen as if this were news.
The mason tells her not to worry, the worst
is yet to come—and they all laugh together.
He says his ancestors said that theirs
carted the chapel's stone, and yet they ate
miserable onions and old bread,

then there was the time a Nazi,
a kid, put a gun to his head, barked,
and expected him to speak a language
he couldn't possibly have known.

To all this she answers if they've heard
that once she could have shot the Devil,
then leaves. Back at her favorite place,
man and monster pitch into each other,
and her mind sketches the triangle
of waste, appetite, and grace. Serene,
she burns it on the anger in her brain
and lets the sparks, secular and good,
formlessly rain down.

(for Alan Shapiro)

Sabbioneta to Parma

In the corridor outside my compartment,
a washerwoman hooks her elbows on the window
and flips the landscape between her hands.
A black-haired boy with yellow fingernails
talks to his rooster *(Ma cosa vuoi da me?)*
while the young priest reading Tasso wiggles his lips
and a high-breasted girl watches him—
station porters scrubbed our windows
to wipe off smugglers' coded messages.
Slow crabbed vineyards beyond the glass
throb in the plain's unforgiving light,
and cordons of cypress sharpen portions
of green sky. Not much depth here,
no counterinsurgency of things
to plunder a standard night. The planet
sits or sinks in its nervelessness.
Five months from now, snow will braid
the creek beds and vine stumps
while a morning express curves past,
the way the porticoes of Sabbioneta
curved away from us, away from life.
I'm one more passionate bystander.
It seems simple enough. Silence, work,
accident, that's really all there is.
Sunslats keel and slice through poplars,
trunk hacked from soil, spindled crown
a stranger to its branches. If I could see
everything, I'd probably go crazy.
There's an ox pulling a man.
There's water running in a ditch.

To My Old City

You're still there in the spectral impress,
the plied grid of trucks and buses,

diesel fume and bloodspoor streaked
on wet streets, cars biting evening papers

from the black newsstand. The trestle's gravel bed
hums above, expectantly, or with relief,

and broken needles of snow, at rest
on silver rails, flash in the coming dark,

while everywhere your hungry light still tries
to reconstruct itself, charm the space

in and around the loose-knit ironworks,
winter's checkered yellowings glaring past

the dark. From here, two years later, I see
in your middle distance a trestle stretched

between two courtyard brownstones, the scene
droning deep: a train tears through the gap,

ratcheting the space with green aquatic squares
that flick past like old sluggish film,

each frame a piece of failing, played-back fact,
and the flustered wheels click, mumble, click

in flukes of young snow flailing up around
those strange riders abiding in the glass.

Gulls on Dumps

or broken plastic helmets lost
in screws of punk baling wire

while the sea cries from another time:
a ship balanced on the horizon

but the ledge rose and the ship
resolved into the blue wall behind

until it found its edge again,
and birds creaked overhead. They sing

above cardboard wingbeats flogging
mounds of newsprint, seagreen sacks

vomiting cans, rinds, ripped shoes,
a stiff orange cat, the good stuff

gulls strip and sing, tumbling through
the blistered sun fields—

this bounteous despairing city
the mind inhabits. One thing tells

the story of some other. The sloping song
written above these peppered white hills

in flight above cold swells,
a memory of the sea's deepest place

where blue or green turns black
and millions of transparent lives

school and funnel, feeding, darkling,
until all sister stories pause

in this instant, when the gulls quit
their song, the wind falls, the sea stops.

The Reading

After the fluttered knocks on the near green door,
the room fills with their various lights and flesh.

I know (through smoked glass or gels) most of the faces.
Harry G., who knew me when, ushers them in.

In blue lamplight, my first girlfriend touches her blouse,
the moist nipple there. Around the unfinished circle

my father sits, rubbing his hands, and waits
for some message to appear in them;

he chokes, as usual, on the brink of speech,
worrying his skin instead, while my sister,

grown older than he, custodial, pained and kind,
fails to heal him with her look and touch.

Toward the back I see a runt version of myself,
stubbing a cigarette in my palm. And Cousin Tom

in his motorcycle jacket and silk foulard—
Tommy baby-grins and spits on the rug.

In the bodiless loop and sway of arms and breasts,
the woman of my familiar dream comes close again,

lifting to my mouth a cool wooden bowl of milk.
I reach for her and my hand passes clean through.

She reminds me of what I need to hear,
that the pilgrims in the room or soon to be

have come to listen, that I had better start soon,
before it gets too late and they all decide to leave.

The Cellar Twenty Years Later

The twelve goofed wooden steps
even now try to shrug me off,
as I duck under the lintel,
the cockeyed timber where we nailed
the yellow horseshoe's horns,
tines down, to beat bad luck.

That's how we gave the Devil back
his own smart gilded work.
I passed under this poor man's sign
a hundred times, baffled in its force
stretched tight between upstairs rooms
and dark-shining zones below.

Hugging the wall, I can feel the coal trap
snap and shutter wide, then flint-streams
flashing hauled-in sunshine
cheered down the chute into the bin.
I stood aslant and almost pitched
off the steps into the phaseless dark.

But the horseshoe did its work
and held and saved me from the fall
into mineral gravity's craziness.
It fixed me in this middle range,
a little lost, off balance, listening
to odd faint songs above my head.

Chinese Apples

Autumn's first days whiten words
   puffed into the market air
     by wives clustered like bees
around packing crates splayed
   with pears, green apples, late grapefruit.
     They hover, peck, breathe quick gulps
where hints of lowering sunlight sort out
   the blushed, lacquered pomegranates
     from fruit more common through the year.
We'll watch the kitchen's sharpest blade
   halve the globe, and poke the sharp wick
     pouting from one end,
then sit outside on two-stepped marble stoops
   all alike, like rickshaw men, or ice.
     The sudden bounty: barbed
tart seeds tucked in the honeycomb pulp,
   tiny scoops a child's finger fills
     to squirt the slick pips out,
all our concentration on that force,
   the juice, blood-seeped well water
     shining in every cell.
Deeper inside its silky chambers
   the girl waits, unmoving, filled
     with heavy seeds
she took too eagerly—she can't move, pressed
   by the darker god-weight
     while her mother grieves
and sears and blights the grain, with a word
   turns juice and husk to dust.
     But now, in fall, in the carved

glistening belly of Chinese apples, Persephone
   rises again, for a while, her marriage bed's
     honeyed reek dripping
from her cool hands. We children swarm
   at her fingertips, licking her nectar,
     chilled and giggling for more.

The Divine

The night sea's broken forms,
its long torn hush,
erase every recent trace
like wind to dust.

In the scrublight, another's
sharp footprints mix
with black sand, the tide's scrawl
over weeds and sticks.

My voice going out has nothing
new to say, no slight
shock of self to lend
a world hammered soft tonight.

Teach me not to love
the flattery of foam
and salt. Teach me to learn
I have nothing of my own.

I-80

Across the baked black lengths of Kansas, west of Salina,
cottonwoods whisking close to culverts and stream beds
seemed to nod in memory to what the settlers saw:
pacific grass shaving tops of wagon wheels, a horizon
tide of buffalo in late spring heat, wiggling swathes
cut by jackrabbits through devil's claw and thistle,
sovereignties soon thinned out by the iron god of work.

Planting was a different kind of worship, fated and impious
in ways they'd never understand. Hungry for the quick,
high yield, they ploughed too often deep into nested
grass roots, shearing binders that kept the land compact.
The soil loosened into continents of dirt
waiting for a wind to scoop and pitch the prairie
in black swells that wiped out earth and sky.

For us, driving west, the blacktop simmered;
the road sagged from sun fatigue. On the horizon,
too far to judge their distance, grain elevators oozed.
"When I was a girl," you said, "we called them
prairie skyscrapers, so we could think we were a city."
"Or monster organ pipes. The B Minor Mass or something?"
"Too liturgical, and Roman, for this part of the state."

For you, passing through your country after ten lost years,
the return was swallowed whole by that voluptuary wind
raking tumbleweed through neat rows of winter wheat sprouts,
the daddy longlegs irrigation rigs blessing crops

with water sucked from the sinking table underground,
a solemn trim geometry scrambled by occasional feedlots,
bellowing mud, and shrouded tire-weighted fodder dumps.

You tried to shake free from that at the Great Divide.
At eleven thousand feet, locking arms, dizzied,
we looked into the sandstone layers, the eroded revisions
like broken graphs that made you wish for your discursive plains.
Our jittery talk trickled over the rim's orange ring-stacks
until a sudden rain absorbed us in the scene. I pronounced
something about it all, something puny and full of myself.

In the Sierras two nights later, you turned in early,
hoping to dream the next day's descent. Three other fires
burned like torches at campsites. I sat stoking ours.
Wind passing through the pines brought crackling phrases
from the other fires, and noise of creatures in the brush,
and your dream-voice like dry twigs catching in the fire,
your words passing through firelight to the treetops.

Then the valley, already browning out, burn-ready,
waiting for winter rain to call back the angry greens;
bean and lettuce fields, redwood, eucalyptus, the sandy glare
of coastland choked with ice plant, sea lion complaint, and you
reading from your book: When religion becomes too orthodox,
its day of inwardness is over, the spring is dry, the hawk is heard
only in a shadow falling across the plain down canyon walls.

Woman Ironing

. . . a city churchyard with moonlight,
headstones, sepulchers like unbaked loaves,
some weeds silvered white,
knobby trees whose little shadows
half blot names channeled in the stones . . .

On your grandmother's pillowcase
—embroidered initials coiled
into the rumpled white field—
the freshened shadow of your head appears,
pressed smooth, steaming briefly.

The One-Year-Old Lemon Tree

Its small celestial reach stops
   where the counterweight, the first
      tough green fruit, pulls earthward
and returns the brazen, almost rank perfume
of blossoms now six months gone.

The slurred odor of its leaves
   calls back that long evening's end:
      we shivered in the cool light
a northerly sun bent against the planet
into the hands of friends

who helped clear our outdoor supper's
   sharp debris—forks, tin plates,
      balled napkins and bone nests.
The lemon blossoms throbbed. The air
slowed with all that young life,

the fragrance quickened in our veins
   the common, too surprising wish
      to hold, just then, someone,
whoever stood nearest, whatever charm
would bind us to the lowering light.

Then someone said, "Let's eat the tree"—
   Rip the bole, raid the green heart,
      devour remembrance with one moment's
hunger, and eat the nature of things.
Scraped plates, laughter, glasses refilled . . .

Our sweet anger urged and gathered us
around the young tree's tub, made us
tamp the wet soil and drink fast
the clear smell of unseen yellow fruit
in time we ourselves might never know.

The Apricot Trees

The toothy limbs pruned in February
lay tangled on the ground, and so their snares
grabbed or clawed or snapped shut where you walked.
One branch bit your thigh, inside, and you
slapped the spot where blood seeped and trailed,
the red slug track pointing toward your belly.

After years of marriage and two years tending
those four trees, our share of remnants left from orchards
that once shaded all these neighborhoods,
the cycle led us to imagine one
uncontested season of preserves and jams
glowing in the cupboard, in the dark.

One bough I hadn't braced in time soon snapped.
Late nights, to reach our door we had to lean,
silent and drunk, around that torn point
then stoop under sagging arcades of fruit,
green, orange, gold succulence of summer
tedium when things ripen too fast and fall.

When friends stumbled away with knobby sacks,
they must have thought it no strange thing that we
would leave this place, each other, the story
of the orchards, that we would give away
perfection's spoils to anyone who asked.
We had enough. Earlier, before the fruit

took form and force in bud, I sliced one branch
to follow tracks laid in the cool moist flesh

by borers I couldn't find. All around
they've left their sign: a stone-glass bubble sealed
to trunk or branch, gemfire flared inside
false, perfectly imagined apricots.

Five Studies

Fast, but mined with a motion, a drift,
And it crowds and it combs to the fall.

The oleanders claw the screen.
Streetlight mattes their shadows
on white shades beside the bed.
Somewhere, out there, Venus sets.
In here, the dim corner lampshade
showers its cone of phosphors,

prickling our arms and legs,
useless, unraveled, waiting for
the next occasion, for tedium
to become desire or something like.
You're dissolving into your white ground.
The oleanders grab the sheets.

———————

The punk, yeasty, summer-rot taste,
confused with autumn's charred air
in the dampened sheets . . .
In another time, in Naples, the bay's
garbage seeped into our high room,
the briny reek of dead fish, grease,

black lemon rinds. And the rattle
of beached voices, boat sirens, car horns,
rising from our swayback bed.
We loved each other too much, loved ourselves

sick because we had it all
and never thought we'd have enough.

———————

Rain finished the streets, blacker
with the traffic light's sulfur breath
flaring under the wheels. We ran the light
to get home faster, take each other's
pulse-beat, tongue and tooth—the rainskin,
night's last images, drying up.

The wipers screeched a few more beats.
We primed the radio's huggy bass:
*No tomorrow will, O baby, always be
for you, for me.* The marginal hills rose
in a haze, too far. We had song
and home. So lost, we held on.

———————

The green mash of husk and pulp
smears long slime-pools on the asphalt.
The curved shades of walnut leaves unframe
the squirrel whose jacked-up, loping arcs
repeat the cadence of the leaves,
a mossy nut between his teeth.

Another plunges from a branch.
The sphere of air cracks, a world-tile

snaps off, spins to a stop.
Everything feels holy, falling.
Another furred stone drops
then spirals up the tree.

I woke in January (the grass already thicker,
greener, a hurt green, and brainy camphor trees
nodding in the low light)—I woke
to frost hazing all that green, the not-white,
not-silver thin beaten breath
on window panes, oleander, windshield, grass,

and green shoots that later bloomed narcissus,
whited heads inclined to their fresh image
nowhere found in the now recurrent frost.
We cut and put them in our oldest
green glass, watched them bend more each day
looking for the frost, there, not there.

FROM

The Restorers

(1992)

The Early Part of the Day

Most of them lean into the windless sun,
stretching their necks a little, like birds,
working to keep in motion, at least that.
They get their exercise walking the street
down from the rehab unit, past my house,
unrighteous, ignoring the sluice of cars,
school kids on bikes, buses heaving people
from the cinder-block slum two blocks beyond
to gardens, pools, and kitchens one suburb away.
Not quite that far, at the new neighborhood park,
the vets, all mental cases, take themselves
before they have to loop back home, a few
dressed out of sync—porkpie hats, bell-bottoms—
but with fanatical composure, or disarray
as if they whipped themselves with clothes that stuck.
Their mild faces sit apart, in twos and threes,
and watch the young, shining wives cheer their children
down the slide and breeze them high on swings.
The homeless, too, love the park, the sunshine,
thick grass, shade if they need it, the safety
of hidden money those wives and children own.
The blacks and Mexicans who ride the bus
don't stop here. Others, sleeping on the grass,
hug swollen plastic sacks. The morning I saw one
clawing a spill of socks, jars, and paper towels,
I recalled the man, a computer engineer,
who stewed in Dickens and ancient history
to keep him thinking, he told me, after being lost
for years "in Uncle Sam's premier nuthouse,"
because after the mine went off, his hearing gone,

he's on his knees scooping together his best friend.
I've never noticed here the one young guy
I'd recognize, I've seen him stalk by so often,
the one whose moral sense I slur with this.
He's out of life, or nearly. In his studious, locked,
unmigratory look, as if scrutinizing
each clear zone of air he has to pass through,
knowing he may never pass that way again,
there's Caravaggio's Thomas, squinty, curious,
humming a little, prying open the moist lips
in his Redeemer's side, puzzling out the fact,
inquisitor of a body divine who hopes to find,
in the meat of the flesh he's touched, a holiness
they've said will bear him to another life.

The Faery Child

Saying his prayers, he hears them scrape their flesh
up from under the bed, their voices solid, animal,
like those his own chimes with all day, the human ones.

Except for their differentness, like fluted air,
wind through tall bending trees, or owl's cry too drawn out.
Their bodies are their voices. They tell him how to live,

that he will soon return with them, to be of them.
Some days they rise behind the sofa—giggles, snorts—
to finger the piano and tap the TV buttons.

You're not of these things, they say, you can't belong
to this, you belong to the voices of our flesh,
our life's yours, we can make you really glad.

Once, swarming through the door screen from the patio,
hurried in their always near breathing voices,
they closed around him, holding hands, locking dark

on darker air, and he knew he could die for them
and live his heart away, at last, for their sounds
that are so beautiful they rip him from his place,

for they won't let the plain, vaporous, half-seen world
exist for him, their presences like pollen dust
on the keys, the screen-door latch, his books and pens.

First time he saw them, from the school window, they were
graygreen scarves, tangled in a bush, that turned
to children grown moment to moment into adults,

and now their voices come like scarves to swaddle him,
untouching, cottony, ravishing him away
from engulfment in some middle, necessary world.

The Museum of Natural History

Dawn rises where the great hall ends.
The water hole's twilight shocking pink
erodes to backstage noises, shapes . . .
The antelope's indifferent head
points its antlers toward a wasp nest's
corrugated skull-heap. The sound track
whines and mixes varieties
of mud's coppery morning song.

And killing ground. The numbed roar
of big cats in the distance cuts through
the other hunger music. Above,
a hooter ridicules creation:
the thirsty me-monkey, the person
snickering nervous in the tree,
waiting to shinny down and drink
from the clear pool, the source, the ditch.

The diorama's temper fades
toward dusk. We move, outrunning
the shriveled time, into the room
where we feel at once all sorts of blood
laboring separate in our veins,
from savanna's matinal light
to stinking rock moss and pit slime.
The crocodile's muddy blood

pumped twice, a hundred years each time,
whipped its dragon tail to kill
some absent or remembered threat.

Behind, the tortoise was another
blear-veined rock. You turned, stooped,
bent your nose against the glass,
inches from the rattler's head
slung midair from its squat black perch.

I remembered later how you rapped hard,
impatient, at the glass. To startle
or wake the killer's attention?
At lakeside, the blood-drop pricked from rock
was a ladybug's carapace,
flown in a blister of wingbeats
when you drummed your stubby fingertips,
when you drummed your thick red nails.

Adam's Garden

Walking home, I saw them
matched up near the tree,
my shy mud-faced drudge
and anxious golden boy,
and could have yelled both back
when I saw his raised hand
swollen through the club,
his fist an oak knob, flesh
gone to green wood,
the whole tree shrieking outraged
offering. That's all.
Blood-puddles at its roots,
under a clear sky,
the tree's still growing.

It's like the blazing stalk
the Angel held, at the rent
in the moist green wall,
pointing out our new work.
Diggers, dung-gatherers,
root-eaters—what else?
He says things could be worse.
He says he killed my other son.
He and I know our place,

work-pit, dirt, so lovely when
moonlight lies like cuttings,
like white ashes everywhere,
God's boneyard we tend
not far from the other gate.

(After Tintoretto's Cain and Abel*)*

Starlings

Snarls, bread trucks, yeast
breathing inside huddled bags,
and sleepers completing lives
behind their gray windows.

A whistle on the phone wires,
feathers, twitches, whistling
down to the hot loaves.

Reeds everywhere, pulse,
flesh, flutes, and wakened sighs.
An answer. Radio news

and breathers behind our windows,
birds' new voices changing,
changed, to the unforgiving
hunger screech of immigrants.

Poem

Your features in the opaque votary
cringe with rain
that scores image and headstone,
sluicing channels underground.
A mild look that seems
to want other knowledge,
the fair oblivion of the ditch,
of hair, ash, and bone.
In your half-smile, half-knowledge
the photographer found
in scuffed studio light:
stars' distance, starlight's nearness,
your fingers touching a man's hair,
your kiss on a child's forehead,
your throat and breast aflame
when someone noticed you.

This token image, saving that,
gives up everything else.
The heavenward mind
that sees gods and goats in starlines
rots in the ground.

Where's deity in mud and metals?
Heads in the clouds, we live
underworld, boneless shades
imagining ourselves real.

Staring off to one side,
desirous, bemused,
for you existence was liturgy,
the god-wish in your look,
your gestures, skull, and dust.
Rainwater cuts that presence,
following you down.

(After Leopardi's Sopra il ritratto di una bella donna)

Gethsemane

Judas, unlike us, had the nerve to follow,
dogging His heels, for what? To learn
a new vocabulary, a mystery-prayer,
down there in yellow iris that smelled
like carcass? He came back smiling.
The dog had its day, rolling in meat.
The meat was news: the Word of God
wants what we want, to be unchosen.

Did he make up his own mind?
What if he said, I don't see Him here,
let's check later? Instead he gagged on words,
as if his mouth brimmed with water
brought from the garden: *Blood squirms*
from blossom loads and cracked boughs,
and in the stagnant lake of the heart
the sprouting trunk splits, groans,
spilling wine, the spongy dirt
inhales any blood that falls,
and I'm falling into the tree
and dogs at lakeside bark at clouds . . .

Like that. As if his own speech could
infuriate time while he waited to act,
or have the betrayal merely happen
(as joy sometimes merely happens).
But the soldiers got impatient,
so finally his bloodless lips
screamed *More life! More salt!*
before he gave away his kiss.

Emmaus

The way he offered things
was first to take them from you.
You can (he seemed to say)
possess all life, but give me
all you will ever want.

The knife, the cup, the bread,
he grabbed them without a word,
to house the sense we had
of miraculous contagion.
His goodwill hissed like rage.

And then I thought he spoke.
But that was heat pulsing
from nerveless, mudgray flesh,
and a humming all around him
that I've felt in lightning storms.

We met his affronted silence
with an empire's keen, belched noise,
the humble oohs and grunts
that mocked his outraged offer
to burn old lives away.

Holding out the bread,
he pointed at my ripped sleeve,
and his curt thanks for bounty,
his first words, were laid
along the knife's tough blade.

To eat of bread he touched,
to taste those angry words,
changed the feel of time.
That's how I knew, at last,
he had come back for us

whose anger measures love.
When he left—where he was,
he wasn't—we too gave thanks
for the heat-sick wind and rain
drummed up in his absence.

We argued half the night,
drunk with explanations.
We'd known whose god he was.
Now we knew what kind. For love,
we ate our own green want.

Poem

The grass bundle the girl
brings back from the fields
ignites flakes of sundown falling from her shoulders
to the violets and roses in her fist.
Sunday flowers, the kind she'll pin
to her hair and bodice.
Out front, huddled with her cronies,
somebody's maiden aunt holds the spot
still warmed by late light:
she's unpacking the same old story,
her own lost time when, still lean and quick,
every Sunday she dressed up
and danced all night with men she knew
in that old perfection.

It's already getting dark,
the sky's sober blue comes back;
in moonlight's newest candor, shadows hurry down
from the hills and rooftops.
Church bells bang out tomorrow's news—
no work, no work. Hearing that,
we'd say the news, for once, sounds good.
Boys foam into the little piazza,
leapfrogging flagstones, their shrieks
like wind flaying the field hand walking by,
shouldering a hoe, headed toward
his lard and lentils supper,
toward Sunday, when he can pause.
    Then everything's quiet.
The lights go out. That's when we hear

the hammer and saw, the carpenter
pushing all night
to finish a job by the oil lamp
before dawn breaks.
   The best of seven,
Saturday's engorged with wish and joy;
tomorrow's time ripens
dread and sadness—
by then we're already crushed by work
we know we'll have to do.
   But none of that
for you, sunny child;
you can drown in happiness
and breathe the sweet day's season
of existence. If you're lucky,
no Sunday joy
will sicken you too soon.

(After Leopardi's Il sabato del villaggio)

Augustine on the Beach

The tide speeds up. The sun chills down.
The local drifter in his crushed straw hat
shuffles toward the funneled hole:
for days now, a chubby ten-year-old
kneels, digs, dumping buckets of sea
into the pit, back and forth,
surf to beach, smudging prints
left by busy sandpipers.
Nothing changes. The hobo, yelling,
flags his hat. They rehearse the script.
The dirigible's dragon shade
absorbs us. The calm boy explains
he's "working the ocean," that soon
he'll finally have it emptied out.
The other, like a wild parent,
shouts not to waste his life
repeating mysteries of faith.
The big baby fumbles pail and sand.
The man says, has already said
all the days I've been witness here,
to look out there, at those sea lions
watching us, intent, undesirous,
beyond the agonized sea spray
that shouts for us from the rocks.

St. Francis of Assisi

The View

The plain's hatching
after rainless months.

A dust devil rips
a peach orchard

down there, a seam snuffed
by falling dust-fruit.

Behind the vine rows'
shriveled abundance

a low fire runs
ragged by the ditch

like voided skins
waving back at us.

September, thirsting,
sings our Hosannah,

shrieks red poverties
to old heaven's eye.

1944

You want February? Snow and sleet came down hard,
heaven's post-Christmas gift to freeze our eyelids shut.
Walking the icy ground, our shoes all shot with holes,
we did the Alexander's Army Ragtime Dance,
stomping snow off bones safely packed in newspapers.
From down below, we must have looked crazy happy,
dancing like Hollywood Indians, though who had
anything to eat? We dreamed lard. The wolves came,
not straight into town, not into the piazza
but near the outcrop behind the church. God's design,
the best—the way they study the tired world
makes them next to human. They're waiting
while they move. I'd worship that expectancy.
If I could talk to one, just a few minutes,
he'd teach me hunger's secrets. So one awful night
I wrapped my legs and feet, stuffed more papers inside
pants and shirt, then danced my way behind the church.
Faint gray writing on the snow. Skin and bones, sneezes,
frost feathers, drifting away. Two of them walked back,
canny big-shot archbishop warrior types. They said:
The moon's blue, we know you want secrets, advice,
news from this side. Our truth is: Forget likenesses,
live inside your carbon soul, the moon's black and blue,
in the soul's time the world's one winter together.

Renunciation

The snowy poplar seeds are everywhere,
balling against curbs and car wheels,

sifting through gates, doorways, kitchen windows,
snagged by white blossoms shaken loose

from the nodding horse-chestnut leaves. We stand
in their shadows—our springtime's dark.

The debris scrapes our cheeks, clings an instant
to our lashes, chokes the soft breath

before tumbling off the near precipice.
We want divine uncertainty.

O give us the Judas tree's blood shadows,
make us sick with rank pear blossoms,

blind us with earth's random pieces engorged
with broom's milky fallen sun-flesh.

The Restorers

(Strozzi Chapel, Santa Maria Novella)

*S. Philip was taken of the paynims, which would constrain
him to make sacrifice to an idol, and anon under the idol
issued a right, great dragon, and the dragon corrupted the
people with breath that they were all sick.*

Backlit shades groan through the green nets,
trailing voices along the scaffold's bones.
*A sweet roll maybe.   Water!   It's too cold.
And coffee, sure.*   On the next, just-finished wall
the demon, a knotty razorback muscle,
explodes the altar's marble base and squirms
at Philip's feet. The saint, looking down,
points up at Mars upon his glassy perch
jabbing a snaggled lance at that old heaven—
pilasters braced by 3-D breastplates,
greaves, smashed racking wheels, the god's place
engorged with flags, amphorae, empire's
crabbed junkwares to thicken the inaction.
Courtiers, soldiers, burnt-out believers,
huddle both sides of the altar's
detonated symmetries.

A small Redeemer, smeared top right
in an afterthought of sunshine,
drags his cross toward those sea-voices
crooning behind their mask. *Look at this.*

It's cold enough.   Handiwork, to reclaim
or fulfill some memory print.   *See?*
Filippino's style already restored
in this image of the high priest's son,
stung by the dragon, dying in a merchant's arms.
A century's discipline of hard outline
sags into quivering drapes and folds,
the suffered exactitudes of flesh
now sketchy wrappers, brocades,
ringlet mops roughed and melting
around identical faces. The wall
weeps carnal stress into mere effects.

At my back, an answering noise.
Whispers quizzing the chilled
vacancy of our atonements.
The three teenage girls, hand in hand,
are Graces dancing a shaggy circle
before Masaccio's *Trinity.*
Their interrogating voices slash
the mystery painted into the wall;
dates, technique, influence.
The long, blood-ripened God endures
at one center of one history,
housed, kept, more by imagination
than belief, before voluptuous form
trembled into the nerve ends of style.
The girls genuflect, cross themselves,
stinging the space with energetic facts,

then come this way, hunched and leggy
in their wrinkled coats, clapping florid
gumball-colored gloves, a winter's version
of the image Filippino's teacher made.
They also bring a winter quiet—
there's less to say of the lesser painter.
No worship, no signs, fewer facts.
They act out one passage
and pinch their noses like two figures
in the plaster—only the bulky monster's saved
from nervous drawing. Every word dies
in warm vapors streaming from their lips.
Look here. More water now. They wheeze
laughter through their gloves. Others join us,
aiming cameras at the trembling screen.
Not too much. Not too much this time.

We're stuck there, unformed, unfinished,
in time to see the monster driven out.
Less fearful at the latecomer's wall,
the girl whose long, fine-spun curls
brighten the bitter air around her head
talks back to the high secret voices:
"That's hard work, isn't it? And it's
so cold!" *Not so hard.* "Save it all."
It just takes time. "For us." *You know?*
"Whatever it is." Someone snaps a picture.
We're still in it, breathing, worlds away

from what Masaccio knew, and turned away
from Philip's scene, too, whose images
our own forms imitate. We're smiling
up toward the floating shades, the voices,
the steady light mashed in the covering web.

The Hotel Room Mirror

But who was it, then, that made her so unhappy?

—Madame Bovary

A half-room, foreshortened even more
in the huge speckled armoire glass,
the distance chopped, uncrossable,
between your image and where I stood

twiddling the doorknob before I knew
my own key didn't fit, late night,
your interior so underlit
that bluer shadows oozed your forms.

Already too late, the door
breezed open where your back and thighs
twisted in the green-winged chair,
your body's light coiled, at rest.

Dressed, angled deeper in the surface,
your man pleaded, hands wide, as he flexed
sharp from the bed's protesting edge,
the sheets pinwheeled beneath his weight.

Your glance and his (haphazard,
stark and unconcerned) found mine
in the frame, waiting, though I stayed
invisible to myself, my stare

like your bold forms inhabiting
our depth of field, in the scuffed glass
transcribed. It was already still
too late to save you or be saved.

In Calabria

The fish-bone husband, aslant
behind her paddling hands, checked our plates
then nosed back toward the kitchen.
She stood watching with us;
just beyond the terrace rail,
bare-chested men hooted their sons
from the cabin boat listing on chocks
that gouged a crooked trench
toward the small, noiseless surf.

Still Greeks, she said. Sea salt
in their blood, gills and seaweed
for brains sometimes. Boys love it.
We tried once to open a place
back home. Wrong home. Landlocked,
half-dunce for the weird language,
my husband had to bring us back.
Reverend Paisley used to stop
and take a bowl of soup. A bad man then,

a bad man now, visiting his mum.
The plump hands shooed her words
the way she shooed the boat, and boys,
from our terrace, down toward the sea.
Now that's all past. Now is now.
The men peg down the boat, throw ropes
on their shoulders, and walk away,
shouting at the skinny boys
to get back, be good, come on home.

You get such a lousy share
once the broker takes his cut—
a young family, two houses down,
brought swordfish straight to market.
The bonfire, the black-smoke
gasoline stench their boats made,
was like Ulster, like cars. Scorch marks
chip the water while she speaks.
The sea-bound dark thins out.

A few Formica tables, and customers,
her husband checking plates. Her arms
sweep the terrace: So after Ireland
we took this; it's still too small.
But when we're ready to expand,
the landlord, a nice man, tells us
someone won't be happy. The world
belongs to always someone else.
The full moon breaks the sea.

Above invisible boats, farther out,
fuzzed lanterns dangle, while the reaper
rows a wide quiet circle.
On nights like this, she says,
the anchovies swim toward light
if it's quiet. It's their turn,
because the great one, the swordfish,
can't be caught, so they say,
because the moon's not right.

The Sicilian Vespers

(Teatro Comunale, Bologna, 1986)

A batwing shadow stroked the boxes.
The final act, when wedding bells
toll love's bridal part in slaughter—
orange groves, blue sky, then peasants
erupt and kill the well-fed French.
("The heart's cry, yes!") They kill some more,
whoever's there. ("Vengeance! Vengeance!")
The baton batwinged from the pit,
and we swayed to its call. The pensioners,
old trade unionists, wept and cheered.
Provincial Verdi, dying in his room,
hears from the straw-decked streets below
the muffled hoofbeats, a village band,
its oompah brass and drum, love's mallet
beating time to blood. We fluttered
the exits in one another's arms.

The New Year's air outside gagged us.
The gypsies grabbed at us while we gossiped
through the sleet, scarves mashed to our lips.
Graffiti, chalky blue-gray spooks,
bled down the theater's orange walls.
Luscious fake orange trees. Scythes, picks.
Nineteen-hundred. The high room's deathbed.
The lovers' finest task, they think,
is to outsing each other's grief.
Viva la guerra, viva l'amore.
The gypsies wanted more from us.

Their hungry shadows tossed with ours
against the walls. Artisans, thieves,
shopkeepers, and street people trashed
the governor's palace that once stood here.
They picked it clean. Its timbers and stone

still brace houses all over town.
In '68, on opening night,
students pelted the black-tie crowd—
unreal love-and-death contraptions,
overpriced nostalgia, stage tricks
in place of brute cheap history.
We die, or kill, or let be killed,
then wake to other minor terror,
to our intensest selves—angels,
blood and guts, images, facts.
Six years ago, at the railroad station,
sweethearts, summer help, sons, whoever,
traveling second class, were killed
by satchel bombs in a waiting room.
Which of them caught a smell of oranges?
Or saw real bats flying from distant lofts?

Poem

A few bedroom lights.
The moon in windless apple trees
shines across the rooftops,
picking apart hills, empty streets . . .
You're above it all,
sleeping in your room.
No night sweats or pulsing throat,
no shiver when world-stuff sags,
estranged, unfelt, yet smothers anyway
if love fails in us.
You'll sleep off today's
alcohol flush, the shadow-twitch
of too much dancing,
dreaming back to implausible grins
pimply boys hung on you
before you dumped them in the pit
of your voluptuous indifference. You're watching yourself
smile in that dream. I'm down here, shrill as always,
counting off days in my green time.
Our bachelor locksmith in the corner house
sings through his boozy haze.
He's always alone.
Does anything leave a trace?
I push words around in dirt
tomorrow's rain ploughs under.
Holiday, workday. Wool mills clatter
Goethe's "inhuman noise." Jackboots
plough down Rome's gaunt armies.
Achilles howls at blood he needs to taste.
Behind a shutter on our quiet street,

Augustine sobs into his books.
When I was young, full of myself
and not lost enough to love,
unnerved before some holiday's
solemn terminal bliss,
I buried my head in a pillow.
Late that night, someone else's song
turning and fading around a corner
called me, and calls me now,
caught long gone in my throat.

(*After Leopardi's* La sera del dì di festa)

Near Damascus

The antlered scarab rolled a dung ball
for its brood; a red ant, tipsy,
bulldozed a flinty wedge of chaff.
Mud slots caused by recent rain,
crusted over by the heat—
moon mountains seen close up; my mouth
plugged with road grit and surprise
just when I tried to shout *no*
to the blunt lightning spike that stopped me . . .

In the mountains of the moon I saw
a wasp dragging a grasshopper
to a frothing nest, grubs lingering
through their episode, and larvae
I'd have chewed like honeycomb
if it would have saved my sight.
Antaeus inhaled force from dirt;
he was luckier, never much
for visions, and too far gone.

In my head, I see this body
dumped flat. Painted in above,
the horse twists and straddles me,
his eyes flare, ecstatic, new,
contemptuous of the thing that fell,
while the light shaft curries his flank
and nails me down, the unloved me,
rousted, found out, blasted, saved
down in the road's pearly filth.

Old Gold

Maytime pepper plants and geraniums
on scabby balconies. Socks and panties
clocking the breeze. Everything's open.
A hurt peal breaks from a TV
and sails down curbside . . .

Then another season. Indian summer:
love's betrayal, someone else's trouble
choking from a high window
earnest and off-key. I go walking
to want just that, at all hours, shaky

and too serious in the narrow streets
of my foreign city. It's no way home.
Once I heard a nest, up there
in a tenement, crackle and catch fire,
several voices up in flames.

Now it's winter and tonight
the streets are empty,
windows shut against snow
no one expected, that falls
like a blessing we can breathe.

A car hums past,
driver and his girl smoldering
in the dash lights. A street sweeper
scythes her broom across the snow,
snagging wrappers and dog turds.

The gypsy rosebud girl
pauses inside the tavern door,
to catch secrets or guess
who won't buy. We pause, too,
looking up from our food.

The African with her tonight
calls for *the big boss, the boss man,*
stomping, rattling his velvet shield
of watches, key chains, gold leaf
Eiffel Tower lighters.

A waiter grabs his elbow
and smiles him back outside.
He's the one I saw, the one
I think I saw, later that night
swept by headlights that flayed

a reckless smile from his trapped,
servile fearlessness,
where he squatted and picked the sun's
shattered barrettes and money clips
half-sunken in the snow.

The Original Rhinestone Cowboy

is saying, moments after the rainstorm, that he can ignite
ruby and sapphire scales, gemstone chips of every kind,
by picking his guitar, filling his fist with notes,
then tossing a wedding arcade over all our heads:
I'm dreaming jewels for you people. Here they go!
His knobby hands conduct the burger stand's neon buzz,
the day's last light, green and violet sparks (Take them!)
fluttering down last-ditch yellow, delta red marbled
under car wheels, in oil-slick backwater
we can see offshore. He tells this dream with fact.
He is the original only one. Accept no imitations.
He is homeless, plain unhoused, but glad to be.
His benediction, falling on us who pause to hear,
tips our ears and lashes, returns us to the Garden,
our idea of it at least; we can already taste
the finite shudderings of what was left to us.

His guitar, he says, is a democracy of good intent,
and if some nights it's not so good, that's all right too.
Cars swing into the lot, nick bags from the pickup window
and slide away. Headlights prick tintype sequins
dripping from his buckskin. He gestures down the strip,
to Foster Freeze, U-Haul, Mr. Chicken, used-car domes:
I want you all to dream of being commonwealth,
united in a rhinestone resurrection, proud,
for we're all Americans and have worse things in store.
Trucks grinding toward the interstate toot twice for luck.
He waves: I'm someone who's not going someplace else,

I'm an original, I don't travel too well.
To the rain-smeared cars, the strip, the truckers, to us,
he confers the rest of nothing's colors in his hands:
Bless you children. Fear not the rain. I say
bless you all. The O.R.C. says just you wait.

Three Poems

1.

More conclusions. Moonlight, moonshine,
another year done, under a blue moon.
Eve's puffed, eyeless face pleads
for unconsciousness. Adam's already
a mineral stalk with sex and legs.
We want to remember everything,
track senseless piecemeal moments
into keen incoherence. That's our trouble.
Who needs to remember anything?
We catch sight of ourselves at night
stumbling into a bush, my shade
mothed across yours. My birthday month,
December's lunar completeness—
we remember when we were young,
still unknown to ourselves, unfinished
now more than ever. In our happiest moments
we think it's wisdom to call back
any pain that freezes us in place.

2.

Heartsick, settled for good,
you think you finally know something . . .
You had what seemed to last,
one more false thing.
You drank hope for its thrill,
but believed in it. Now belief
burns off with the thrill.
You could live with, even love,
the way things seemed.
Words were all part of the plot.
You worked. Is anything really worth
the will and rage and trouble?
Life galls and bleeds us dry.
What's left? This world, our slime.
So, give it up one last time.
The species ends in each of us.
Nature's brute force, malingering,
outlives us and makes the world
a common grave and everything
an inexpressible emptiness.

3.

It now feels like a world beyond:
all this, my favorite hill, the hedge
blocking the horizon's better part . . .
My mind roughs out the rest, farther,
where space doesn't stop, and silence
expands like harmless numb dreamtime.
My heart catches at the thought.
The vacant plenty I imagine
runs with the wind storming these trees;
then I invite eternity, the lost seasons,
my own moment's noise. I exist
to crack the perfect image,
the thing I love, then lose it
in the sumptuous chaos of my heart.

> *(After Leopardi's* Alla luna,
> A se stesso, *and* L'infinito*)*

Frankie's Birthday Party

Atlantic City's littlest Bedouin, he says,
and his wife turns toward him, as if she knows
where it's bound to end. I was, I swear to God,
the littlest transfixed Arab, bandaged in towels
so that the sand wouldn't contaminate my skin,
and all those greased thighs and arms around me
made it worse: grown-ups looked as if they squirmed
wet from some fat mother. On the boardwalk,
I shook hands with Mr. Peanut; remember, honey,
my telling you that? The Steel Pier's Diving Horse
kaboomed the water tank. The taffy machine
cranked sexy pink cables—*it* could eat *you,*
I swear, and give you nightmares of jelly pillows
grabbing like rubber breakers or flesh.

"He wakes up," she tells us, smiling straight at him,
"grunting, and like he's punching back invisible walls:
Get these fucking things away, give me air!"
I see that child of myself, he says,
and know he never died, and yet I want him
as if he belonged to someone else. Those kids
on Ninth Street, bagging tomatoes and hauling crates—
their muscles twitch like horseflesh. Ten years I'm gone,
and they're still competing, trading epithets
like Homer's princes, or almost like: one guy yells
to the general crowd, *Your Siamese pigskin mother!*
Another, three stalls down, shouts back: *Your Mongolian
Pekinese Plasticine mother!*
                              "And now,
can you believe it? Philadelphia's only Bedouin

becomes, at an advanced age, a humdinger historian."
But she's the only one not from our place.
She says that as if to cool the story of return.
We could get lost. French fries in paper cones,
grease slicking our fingers like suntan oil;
blinking Pokerino screens, The Wild Mouse, quoits;
and back home, the glittering peacock fan
from fireplugs in August, Death Box bottle-caps
on tacky streets. Now—the voice quickens—
my mother grabs the gambler's shuttle on weekends
to blow her pension on the slots. She'll never learn.

The cake, after pizza, tastes so sweet and sluggish
we breathe through our mouths and cool the thirst
with more beer. He smiled through the song, his wife
holding his hand between both of hers,
but he's not eating, hasn't been. When he picks up,
it sounds like more of the same, his voice clear,
becalmed, the air combed loose with candle smoke,
that in the other time he won't forget,
no more than he'd forget the sun and sand,
it was fun to be last man out and torch a village.
Not to watch it, but to do it, leave it,
then you never wanted to see it again. You lost it.
That part, too, comes back; not the sickening fear,
but the knowledge that fun is what it truly was.

FROM

Shadows Burning

(1995)

Shrine with Flowers

1.

She squeezes sideways
through the screen door,
small knobby apples
slung in her apron
bump her knees and thighs,
five years of drought
but a sort of harvest
or gift, at least
I feel it to be so
when her hands open,
fruit crashing
into the sink,
and her apron disappears.

2.

After the chemo sessions,
my neighbor's wife retreats
to bed and fear,
while across the fence
he and I talk above
a vagrant cavernous smell
of old camphor leaves.
But he's fingering
the plum tree graft
where years ago he sheathed
new bud into old stock,
wedded, barked over,
toughened every season.
We'll have fruit, real sweet,
he says, grinding his thumb
at the splice. Really
good dark black purple.

3.

It's all haywire,
(her old letter still
sweating in my pocket
as I double dig a patch
as per her command)
your heart. Can't you
stop working, or "work"
at knowing yourself?
You act as if acting
matters. Just stop.
House finches doubling
down to a branch
mating for life
while the grinding
orange poppies open
through the rusting
chain-link fence that
defines this ditch.

4.

A sunny wind,
her eyelash
scraping my cheek.
And familiar words
housed in her breath.
Habit and talk,
rose petals, ice,
scent of apples,
laughter tilted back
in her mouth,
even when she
comes home after
visiting next door.
What do we hold
so loosely in common?
Crows in the seedy patch.
Treetops moved by wind.
The shivering tips of grass.

5.

Walking their dainty wrestler's walk, the coons came for Nick's corn, and tore up some lettuce and beans, too. (One found pet rabbits three houses down, lifted the latch and climbed inside the cage, crouching there before it killed.) So he designed and built wood steel-mesh traps. The coons mocked the prototype, they stole the bait, sprung the trapdoor and ran free, then tore up more garden and knocked over the garbage. The revised design worked. While Luisa kept records of her painkillers and watched TV, bored to panic by soaps, game shows, and all that scripted hilarity and dismay, Nick transported the trapped raccoons fifteen miles up into the redwoods above skyline road where the hills start to slope down to the ocean. "This way, they won't come back, you don't have to kill them."

6.

Roses on the table,
how many days, drooping
late March red roses
left out too long
for our small pleasure.
Smelling of old beer,
like my first house,
the blurred men home
late from the taproom,
who pitched like shades
across the TV screen,
blue men, blue vase,
this cloud-ware cube
painted with vague
welkin roses, phantom
blooms that last longer,
rising toward the real
flopped red petals,
my father's pockets
turned inside out.

7.

"What's for dinner?" she asks.
Coon tails and tofu tiramisu
à la California. No kidding.
So we tend our cakey garden
another hour, pulling weeds
we overspent our water rations
to prime last spring. A chilly
fall evening, a shorter day.
The cosmos are blaring.
Peppery nasturtiums
melt on our tongues,
while morning glories
snarl the chain-link.
Why didn't we think
to plant cucumbers or squash
or entreat house finches
to bring us cantaloupe?
Why dig and kill our backs
to cultivate these gauds
so unlike our own flesh?

8.

Clearing green trash in the backyard, I thought I'd go next door and
say something to Luisa, anything, knowing that mostly I'd just
be pushing words around to testify or console, make small talk,
make a sentence. The camphor leaves I grabbed behind the bird-
of-paradise—a rain mould pitted their alarmed beaked flowers—
crumbled in my gloves. The leaves were papery and dim, but that
chilly odor broke from them, and then I'm in my childhood bed with
pneumonia while the vaporizer steams, studying Blue Book reports
on UFOs—Sid Caesar purses his lips before station break, some-
where in the house my father is bashfully drunk. Language is falling
into senselessness like leaves. It has always felt like accidents of
meaning, I'm recalling, the world made over in a casual coincidence
of noises that are words. I held them in my crummy gloves, two sea-
sons of fallen camphor leaves, Luisa's protocols overlapping them.
Now she's getting radiation for the pain and fusses over the wig she
never wears around the house, though most days I hear her holler-
ing from the back door: "Nick, what are you doing now?" I spent
a week trying to control the blackberry. ("Do you ever hear your-
self? *Control.*") It shot up and climbed across the pavement, up
and through the chain-link, then into the rotten shed, prizing under
its boards and ribs and around the skinny plum trees. Blackberries
so sweet after a rainy season that they hurt your teeth and make
children tear their arms on brambles to get at the fruit so that they
can eat themselves sick.

9.

"Takes one to know one,"
she says, while the wind
grazing our bare backs
lifts the roses' perfume
and blows it through weeds
we're pulling like mad.
Then the grass shifts
direction, tree shadows
jerk across the house,
rose blooms knock heads.
We're looking for something,
but what? Shadow of what?
"Gone with the wind, kiddo."

10.

Tonight the grass gets
a dusting sort of rain
that reminds me of drought.
One night last winter, I walked
near South Philly's oilworks,
the ghoulish streetlights dusted
the shaggy boys I heard
("Give it up, asshole!")
before I saw them shuffling
under the schoolyard hoop,
shades tossing in the dark.
Their grayish moonlight
comes back to me now,
sheeting my point of view
where sluggy, sun-logged,
brief Pacific greens wait
for winter, chilled by shadows
burnt and burning cold.

11.

Luisa, Italian beauty, emigrant
Canada to California (wife of Nicola,
union carpenter, called Marchigiani,
of the Marches, emigrant 1950),
attached to the morphine drip
and catheter, in her conscious hours
wants this room where she will die
spotless, tidy as the garden
where the last sweet chard grows.
The mute TV wipes from face
to gunfire to White House lawn.
Nick talks over the pied images
to himself, stands to greet neighbors
who sit an hour or so with her.
Twice he reminds me to take
whatever fruit I find out back.
A few apricots past their prime.
The first figs, mostly green
or purply blue like vein made flesh.
A few hard young mossy peaches,
plus leathery pomegranates,
seeds forcing through the seams
as we force into her bright room
crowding at her side to wait.

12.

The breeze, our bedroom window,
the dark, her breath
tiding at my ear.
The leaves of the plant
whose name I haven't learned
stirring at that sound,
the pitched lift and fall,
while the moon's dense light
pebbles through the leaves
onto her pillow and face,
writing the motion, unselfed.
Wake and tell me, tell me.

                              (for Mary Jane)

Far West

Lilac I never saw
by Watkins Street's housefronts,
die-stamped windows, brick,
the sphinx of granite steps
I rubbed my face against,
smells of roof pitch, dust,
burnt peppers, telephone-
trees, pavements edged
with moss worms, Death Box
chalked on hot blacktop.
Lilac I knew only
in satin color plates
in libraries and once
in flesh at Bartram's Garden,
where sullen, pouchy
Gumbo the Calabrese
drove me from the city
into a late spring twilight,
pointing *(Smell? There?)*
to flowers he didn't name,
until his choppy English
made this: *Are lilacs!*

Now two weeks' chilled
sagging mist grinds
our Pacific mornings,
and it comes to me,
so unlikely, unreal
this far west, it has
its legend, the bland

bluesmoke ceanothus,
"called California lilac."
But what's amazingly here
is Gumbo Bartram's bloom,
barely surviving, throbbing
where there's no right time,
no hard freeze or winter
sleep. In the broken time
I work this out in lines,
in the patch of green behind
this house I do not own,
real lilacs bloom, turn
my head, and go. Leaving,
they are so much with me
that I'm never home again.

The Prayer Mat

Two weeks back east, I read your letter during the news,
our F-15s stitching desert gridpoints, underground fires
out of control, the sky cored by purple smoke jets:
"Bring me (and California) lilacs, or something lilacky.
My meditation's off. The kids that rented after us
tore out those gorgeous lilacs. That made me sick.
I miss you and want you around the house."
Now, your candle's lilac-scented light burns early
with a mockingbird's hysteria in the walnut tree.
Smart bombs still hitting bunkers. Small war, small war.
Liquid pulse mashed TV blue on impact. You meditate
("Not prayer, it's more like thinking") before the flame
and altar stash of bark, acorns, kernels, stones.
State of creation, your thought coursing in I don't know
what star gas torrent of all changes, wanting balance.
More evening news. "Presidents love their video wars,
they love death, they make love with Christmas lights."
Then sleep. You grind your teeth, wring and hack the air.
This morning I walked past your room. Your little shrine's
blueflower smell came again. I picture you trying
to balance there, behind the door, where I can't see.

California Thrasher

Dirt grenades blown around
his big head, he labors
under the lemon tree,
blossom and fruit, bright leaves,
he trenches, he hammers,
he feeds down where
earth's muscled rind wraps
around its molten core,
sea of blue mud flames,
combed fire, swell, cooling foam,
where our dead are waiting,
where we wait ourselves,
he works, hungry, fearless,
our only messenger.

Ice Plant in Bloom

From where I stood at the field's immaculate edge,
walking past an open patch of land that's money bounded,
in California's flat sunlight, by suburban shadows of houses
occupied by professors, dot-comers, lawyers, affluent do-gooders,
simple casual types, plus plumbers, children of lettuce-pickers
and microchip princes, grandchildren of orchard keepers
who pruned and picked apricot trees that covered lot after lot.
Vaporized by money, by the lords and ladies of money,
on one block, three bungalows bulldozed, and the tanky smells
of goatherds and dirt farmers who never got enough water,
held momentarily in the air like an album snapshot's aura,
souls of roller-rink sweethearts and sausage-makers fleeing
heaps of crusty lath, lead pipe, tiny window casements,
then new foundations poured for cozy twelve-room houses.
So what was she doing in that field among weeds and ice plant?
The yellow and pink blooms spiking around her feet like glory?
Cranking her elbow, as surveyors do to distant watchers,
she fanned the air, clouds running low and fast behind her.

A voice seeped through the moodless sunlight
as she seemed to talk to the flowers and high weeds.
She noticed me, pointed in my direction. Accusation, election,
I couldn't tell, or if it was at me myself
or the green undeveloped space she occupied,
welded into her grid by traffic noise. *Okay!*
A word for me? A go-ahead? *Okay!* Smeared by the wind
and maybe not her own voice after all. I held my place.
She could be one of the clenched ministers adrift
in bus terminals and Kmarts, carrying guns
in other parts of America, except she dressed like a lady of money,

snowbird sunglasses, wristwatch like chocolate birthday cake.
The voice, thin and pipey, came from the boy or girl,
blond like her, who edged into view as I watched. The child,
staring down while he cried his song, slowly tread the labyrinth
of ice plant's juicy starburst flesh of leaves. *Okay!*
He follows the space between the flower-bristles at his feet
while the California sky so far from heaven and hell beams down
on us beings of flower, water, and flesh, before we turn to money.
The sky slid through tips of weeds. The sky left us behind.

Red Roses

Five days later,
fuller, heavier,
blown but holding
their overripe pattern,
petals in flight
from the nowhere center . . .

Now longer, two weeks,
and redder, as if
our thought of Eden
raged inside.
What, you said. What
makes them do that?

Crouched over, shoulder
dipping toward the blooms
and their carnal thorns,
you sat up straight
when the earthquake came
that broke buildings in town,

before you bent again
to cut and trim these
to fill our largest vase.
What keeps them with us?
What do they keep?
That perfume soaks the air.

On a Picture by Cézanne

There's no description in the braided stone,
the pear, the stone in the pear, the birchbark,
bread hills on the snowfall tablecloth.
The dog of work gnaws the day's short bone,
snarls a mountainside into lavender and green.
In the mind where objects vanish, almost is all.
Element of pitcher, sky, rockface, blank canvas
plastic and vast in one off-center patch.
To copy what's invisible, to improvise
a soul of things and remake solid life
into fresh anxious unlifelike form.

The Depot

When I was young, they taught us not to ask.
Accept what's there. If you want something else,
or more, don't look too shameful wanting it.
They were too right. Bituminous words,
useless rhyme, cadence, dream structures, plots
to turn life's material fact into sound—
such things helped no one, gave nothing back.
Our mothers scrubbed sidewalks, ironed white shirts
starched upright and sure for school or Mass.
The Infant of Prague balanced his gilded globe
above the TV screen. On Saturdays,
we sat through two coarse-grained double features.
Between times, our fathers worked in steamy plants,
stamped dies, troweled mortar, mixed paint, broke concrete,
carpooled home to beer and shots at Mike's,
a late supper home in silence, then back to Mike's
for night baseball or cards. Our fathers taught us
we had enough. Brick homes, *Your Show of Shows*,
the mothball fleet and flaring oilworks.

I wanted just two things. Rock candy, dyed
rough-cut Easter ruins, useless and real
under the drugstore counter's glass.
And the train set in someone's paneled basement,
its sweet, exact syntax of trestle, track,
village kindness with muggy lights and shops,
the switching yard, semaphores, work sheds,
and depot café where the pharmacist
drinks coffee late tonight. The waitress, Sue,
makes small talk about the pretty snow

that falls along the hills and softens steeples.
The boxcars clack. The coffee urn gurgles.
Under the counter, between stacked plates and cups,
the stink of baccalà soaks the neighborhood;
the sky, held by phone wires, sags with heat
while torn boys, squat and still on the blacktop,
skid bottle-caps from numbered square to square,
avoiding the Death Box, where motion stops,
while Sue's chapped hands unfurl above their heads.

Moving Things

My aunts mentioned her just once,
calling her my aunt, their sister,
though she wasn't. They mentioned
the vinyl recliner in the kitchen,
the "I Like Ike" poster, the Sacred Heart,
cabbage smells, sulfur, and shame.

Before jolted by the gift that called
through but never really for her,
she became unpleasantly calm.
Moments later, after she said
"I don't want this please," God's love
raced down the pulse into her look.

It was as if her things spoke back:
a table leg scraped the floor, a fork
wobbled in a drawer, knickknacks fell.
She nearly died each time it happened.
They said her mind just wasn't there,
or she wasn't in it anymore.

She sat helpless afterward,
papery when they lifted her
from vision seat to bed. The might
to move what her eye fell upon
is the image of her I keep,
her iridescent readiness.

"Buddy's Corner"

The same fake eclairs and Communion cakes adorn D'Ambrosio's window,
now behind bars. Thirty years ago, summer wind burned inside my ears;
bits cribbed from Malory and *Classics Illustrated* crammed my head.
Fireplug spouts erased the air. Kids in alleys swung sticks, bottles—
once I saw them kick a black boy until blood fouled their sneakers.
"You can't hurt rubberheads," our fathers said. Adrift in old facts,
visiting home, I ride the 2 bus into town. At "Buddy's Corner,"
five years in business, the sign's black and white hands clasping
gleam intact. Nobody enters or leaves. Behind D'Ambrosio's counter,
sullen, knowing girls chew gum and watch the street. No one's buying.
When the bus swerves, my head knocks the glass, waking me
to teenage boys in high-tops and fishnet jerseys gliding alongside,
exploding eggs on the windows. Behind me, a girl shrieks.
A woman in cornrows snaps at the driver, "I hate nigger behavior."
On the corner, Kim Park's Everything Store ("We Never Close")
fills the storefront where Rocco's butchershop got bombed
for skimming numbers bets. Tomatoes, apples, lettuce, stacked
in pristine orders. The owner, arms crossed, glares from the door.
Next stop, the Baptist church, where happy noise banned from our liturgy
lifted shout and response, God on the tongue, waiting there for us.
Here to there, we pass brick-pointed houses, brass door knockers,
potted shrubs, window boxes blooming between white shutters,
then punched sheet-metal doors and windows, upended granite steps,
brick moss, weeds like scarecrow straw sprung from cracks in walls.
Old men on stoops are shouting not to make trouble, be cool, act right.
Next to us, afloat between parked cars, the skinny boys stalk the bus,
sifting through tense Korean wives with brown bags and solemn kids.
Our driver, opening the door, rolls past razorwire fence and its church.

The Sleepers

Morning light peaking on City Hall
slants juicy wedges down the stairwells
but can't reach this far underground.
A man grabs air in his fists, panting;
vapors feather from his lips.
"Well fuck me, so then love is what?"
Sniffing, weeping almost, from urine fumes,
he and his friend, suits and ties,
Hall attorneys maybe, turning to leave.
The concourse squirms with sleepers
twisted in cardboard cribs like children
brought home late, pulling covers tighter.
"For her? She says, *Love, Jamie, what's love?*
I say I don't know what either of us is doing."
Subway cars screaming behind the tiled walls
don't wake the breathing heaps of clothes.

William Penn's chalky, sandblasted
hat and face moon above the scaffold racks
that hobble his legs. Two blocks away,
a corporate center's chrome-trimmed seagreen glass
rises higher than Penn's renovated hat.
A woman rubs her gray head against the tiles;
the spot gleams when she totters away,
called back to our life by a boombox
thumping the corridor. Trashy, blood-clotted water
oozing from the walls, streams across the floors
and the sleepers are drowning without a cry.
When I prowled here twenty years ago,
I thought love's better part came from books:

a word was desire's arc from breath
to instinct's needy sound, an *is* or *see*
that might take me out of this life.

A dreamy, ignorant, woozy literalist,
I wanted scenic hardware. Born here,
I'd make my dripping underground
love's pattern for a nice false heaven.
Smoke films the greasy middle air.
The harder I listen, the more Jamie's words
bleed into the echoing hoots, turnstiles,
footsteps, whistles . . . Wet larval streaks
scribble then and now across the floors.
Penn's statue, watertight, gleams above,
custodial, shrunk by the new skyline.
Two bodies curl tight over steaming grates
(one foot withdraws shyly under wraps)
while heels rap past their solemn heads.
We step around the storm-drain seeps, the city
weeps in our tunnels, leaving us alone.

The Mummers

I saw them two days later:
punk parrots strumming banjos
on rooftops, near heaven,
glittering ranks stiff in gilt
sequins and pancake. They marched
off the edge into night space
where phone wires crossed the stars.
Sneakers drooped from starlines.

———————

"Where's the mayor?" "Who needs him?"
Independence Hall
rolls by, buckling in the wind,
tassels bang its skirts.
Silk tents, wedding-cake estates,
Betsy Ross's house.
No music. "He told his cops
to bomb their own town!"

———————

The clowns, ripped and freezing, strut down Broad Street.
The watchers eating breakfast in high rooms look down.
Chickens strut down Broad Street, flasks in their pockets.
The high rooms, dreamed up by the dizzy clowns, approve them.
The watchers daub their children's faces with burnt cork.
The chickens are lilting now from all that cheap rye.
The children, in blackface, want fried chicken for lunch.
The ripped, correct, saved clowns dance all the way downtown.

———————

"One club's warehouse
went up in flames.
Costumes, makeup,
everything. So
they dressed up like
Eskimos but
that New Year's was
the warmest ever."

———————

Saxophones popping frozen spitballs,
drowsy double basses, glockenspiels,
vapors rising from the scrub-board rant.
Below, men sleep in subway tunnels;
rats chew their listing cardboard cribs.
Where's our new hero of the day?
Someone bangs a Korean into a wall
for selling pink carnations on New Year's Day.

———————

When the marchers go
off the edge of rooftops,
the music doesn't stop
inside my head. Winter

stops, the subway roars,
cracking towers flare
behind the roofs. Under
me the sidewalk quakes.

22nd Street

The grass that winter killed was already half-gone with blight or smog. You thought it was funny, that we called our dingy pavement moss "grass." Stiff weeds rising from cracks in the concrete were grass, too. Your singing wasn't nature: it made up for the blight and death and didn't have seasons. Fifties' ballads, early Elvis, Peggy Lee teasers, "Little Tommy Tucker" and "Kyrie Eleison." I listened from my room upstairs on spring days, when the grass was growing and your voice lifted and slid up over street noise. Squirming on your front steps, watching sparrows bop around the sewer grates, you couldn't wait to get going and be a teen. Your songs took me out of my books but became part of them, like initial illustrations, the silvered red vine of your voice separating words and binding them. "Nature hammers us, her children," my poet says, "with sober promises unmade or betrayed." What are we meant for? Making First Communion, I was pious and hortatory, you were shy and bounced your petticoats. What could we have known? A story ages and gets unstable, but facts don't change. Quit business school, made demo tapes, then a husband, drugs, in and out of shelters and recovery units, another husband or two, and in the end the car wreck. Witness or testimony? I don't know my own reason. This feels like another life. Whatever I say, you're not in these words. From your distance, out of nature, not singing.

(after Leopardi's A Sylvia)

154

Ovid in Exile

"Contrition, rhyme, eyelashes, leaders beggaring imagination . . ."
Foul water delirium. Caesar's a junkyard dog
turned on his scrapmetal master, singing master.
A Black Sea resort, bad food, mosquitoes, no wine,
cornpone democracy that makes beggars citizens. Love baits,
teases, poontang scripts, favors he taught girls to beg
from beer-gut industrialists, nothing helps now.
Canny technologue Daedalus warned his febrile son
to stay a middle course, not to burn up or fly low.
Daedalus was right. Sweats and hungers into words,
love's appetite and casual anarchy—
that's no proper world. Poetry wants too much.
His pasty sun sets on bramble farms and clay fields.
Washed up, he needs new subjects, or change of heart.
He has materials: frequent night raids, poison arrows
he's learned to shoot, a wife back home, animal pictures
tortured on her loom. And Augustus, cold war strategist,
peeping at every bedroom window but his own.

The boonies mock a city's fine scales of grit, girls,
sidewalk saxophonists, graffiti, cops, hot food, sugar . . .
You can't say a senator, or his wife, screws dogs
and expect readers to appreciate your style.
Well-bred ironies make you famous and employed.
A poem a day, stale myths, elegiac whining,
whatever cuts contrition's briny taste.
His new friends don't care about his rhymes
or understand his Latin. Shipped back home,
these new poems get him nowhere with bureaucrats.
But he's picking up the phlegmy local language

and tries to make small talk with street vendors.
Learning to be of use, bowlegged, stalking the walls,
helmet raked cockeyed on his heavy, graying head,
when looters cross the plain to storm the so-called town,
he stands with the defenders, crowing his new words,
protecting the only piece of writing he can claim:
stone gardens, malarial fields, trees he can't even name.

Skirts and Slacks

(2001)

Cheap Gold Flats

1. "Philly Babylon"

The bartender tossing cans, carton to cooler,
hand to hand with silky, mortal ease,
while the 4 p.m. beer and shot standees
study the voiceless TV above our heads.
The worst and longest storm on record.
Iceworks canal the pavements, power lines down,
cars pillowed helpless in the snow.
Bus fumes vulcanize the twilight's
911 sirens. Enter HOTSPUR, with alarums,
enter HAZEL, touching my elbow at the bar.
My staticky *Daily News* breaks in the draft.
"What's my horoscope say today, honey?"
Dear Hazel, dear Pisces, don't be hurt,
leave me alone awhile, my mother's dying,
I've been beside her bed for several days,
today she had an extremer monkey look,
her forehead shrunk down to the bucky jaw,
and when she looks above her head, she groans
to see whatever it is she sees, so here,
take my paper, go home, forgive me.

2. Finished Basement

Tonight's big question: What will she
be laid out in? Disco tracks
jump inside the paneling.
Rita loved to dance and so do I.
The sisters, Rachel and Jeanette,
and nieces coming straight from work,
shout across her bed, voicing with
our faithful music in the walls.
Charm bracelet, definitely, the one
she hardly wore, and cheap gold flats
that made her look young and men look twice.
Yackety yak. The unconscious bone
doesn't miss a thing we say,
its used-up flesh helpless
on the pillow. Later, alone with her,
the only noise near me is this new rattle
in her throat. I hear it behind me, too,
the disposal upstairs, a drainpipe clearing,
whatever it is, I feel it coming closer
to finger my hair and stroke my neck.

Skirts and Slacks

The .32 Special,
its Dutch Masters box,
still in their bedroom
closet, days after
my mother's death,
plus my father's
thirty years ago.
I used to practice
disarming, reloading,
putting it in my mouth
for fun. And so,
here it is again,
but (stupid woman,
Great Depression child
scrolling tens and twenties
in macaroni boxes)
loaded, half-cocked.
Oh yes, shoot the burglar
in the closet, the cat
in heat on the fence,
and Calvin Coolidge. She rose,
rammy, close to death,
cocked up in bed
as if pulleyed by heaven,
sometime past midnight.
I was there to watch
her eyes wake for a moment
enraged and hateful toward me.
Bone wooled with slights
of flesh, what certainty

in the body at its end?
And between here and there?
Breath stops, blood fades,
the comic head I'm lifting
from the pillow feels
too merely anatomical
and heavier than before.

Oregon Avenue on a Good Day

Some nights I dream the taste
of pitch and bus fumes and leaf meal
from my old exacting street.
This time home, I'm walking to find

I don't know what. Something always
offers itself while I'm not watching.
I'm hoping for a certain completion,
of house fronts or myself. I don't want

the standard gold of ginkgo leaves,
or weeping cherries, O how beautiful,
but fused presence, a casual fall
of light that strikes and spreads

on enameled aluminum siding, brick,
spangled stonework, fake fieldstone
and clapboard, leftover Santa lights,
casements trimmed in yellow fiberglass,

our common dream of the *all*
and the *only this*, that's exactly
what I can't find. The best of it
is a racy, homely metric unplanned

line to line, building up a scene:
Husband and wife inside, plus kids, suppertime,
pine paneling where scratchy exterior light
rises sweetly above a TV voice.

Leaving Bartram's Garden in Southwest Philadelphia

Outside the gate, the scrawny trees look fine.
New-style trolleys squeak down Woodland
past wasted tycoon mansions and body shops.

There's something I wanted to find,
but what? Roses two months from now
on these brambles? The same refinery fires

lashing over the Schuylkill? The adult hand
that held mine here so many years ago?
None of this happened. Across Spring Garden Bridge,

zoo elephants clicked past my window—
birds jumped from dust igniting on their backs.
Inside Bartram's house, elephant-eared

cure-all pomfrey leaves hung above the hearth.
A redbird gashed the sunned mullioned glass.
I'm in the weave. The brownbrick project softens

in the sun. Stakes in its communal garden catch
seed packets and chip bags blown across the rows.
Tagger signatures surf red and black

across the wall, fearless, dense lines
that conch and muscle so intimately
I can't tell one name from another.

The Apples

The city budget squads have trimmed its hours.
"You can't get in, just go home why don't you."
I couldn't tell how old she was.
Chalky braids crisscrossed her head;
the trench coat bunched around her waist
like paper flowers, her bare legs
streaked pink.
She held a net bag, very French,
filled with cans.

It's equinox.
Sycamore leaves bank at curbs
and blip in bikewheel spokes.
My old library's closed. It's always closed
when I make visits home.
Starlings rake song across the wires.
I used to ride my meaty Schwinn
to this better neighborhood.
"You can't. You can't." She quivered
and chopped the bag against her knee.

Saying that,
I make a mimicry of her.
I learned to do it
in the big, lemony room of floodlit books.
Gg Zz Bb leafed from the walls.
Skyblue globe. Soiled card catalog.
Robinson Crusoe walked across the room,
studying matter, its provisioning use
and weedy homemade powers: I put my feet

into his splayed prints in the sand,
but when he looked behind, he said
Find your own place, kid. Grow up.

You can't you can't. I lost her
in the splintered Sears and Pep Boys doors
down the block, the lost lease sales
and recycling bins.
I feel her words, or think I do,
like matter, plasmic and boreal.
A bus diesels from the curb,
leaves chase its wheels.
Noon light
drenching the tall windows
prints images behind the steel mesh:
clouds crossing sky, stone house fronts,
football rising end over end,
sneakers on power lines like skins
of souls fled or stolen.

Equinox. Measure, middle,
I know I know. All I feel is motion
sucking me in its draft.
The middle's a fiction. I dreamed again
I materialize in the big room,
high ceilings, maybe a sky, the walls
all books sickly organized, but among them
the one true book I'll find by accident.
It will occur to my hands, like Crusoe,
near a textbook's see-through images

of the body's solid veins, muscle mass,
bloodworks and nerve draperies.
It's the book I knew I'd find.

I don't want half-measures. The season
slides to winter. That thought's complete.
Her voice, too, stands watch,
sits, I mean, with me on the cold steps,
while I kill time
reading the book I brought along.
Ruskin, who loved fireflies and unities,
says that the dragon
who guards the golden apples
never sleeps, he hoards them
in his finny coils,
and his greatest skill is mimicry,
mocking human voices,
calling to us in tones
we recognize, until we believe
he's something or someone else.
Then it's too late.

White Blouse White Shirt

Snow falls on the boardwalk
   where they never walked that winter,
street lamps in white boas, surf light
   patching shuttered storefronts.
Where are they? The Ferris wheel
   they once rode looks green.

In this other snapshot
   she wears pedal pushers,
he's in summer whites,
   they swing cigarettes
and hold hands, walking toward me,
   it seems, into breezy life,
where they don't know I'm waiting.
   Now they're renting a rolling chair.
Inside the wicker cowl he says
   "A five-dollar ride, chief."
"It's Chinese, like Charlie Chan."
   Sand buries the sea noise,
resin scents rise from the boards
   into deft sea winds
as they roll past windows larvaed
   with delftware and sable stoles,
licking each other's fingers,
   French fries in paper cones.

When did the boardwalk look like that?
   When was that fresh love?
I stencil redwing blackbirds
   into the scenes, and lilac

brushing window panes, and crocus,
    one garden of one season,
composite, where we look out,
    and between them I become
an hourglass of sand and light
    beside the ocean,
where the sun lets more snow
    fall around our heads.

My Message Left Next to the Phone

I'll leave this where I know you'll look.
Doing seventy across the bridge, I stared too long
at the sun breaking through steelwork cheaters
and saw stiffened shadows, fan blades
pulsing across the fast black surface.
Sailboats flew under me like paper gulls.
What happened then was this: "figures"
from the trusses stepped like nutcrackers,
hundreds, tall and elegant, sexual shadows
scissored into life, gauds flintstruck
from the half-dark and sunlight and panic.

I felt they'd come for me, all that speed,
come to gather me in their motion,
rushed off the bridge into the green bay
with its white sails and weightless hulls waiting.
I was theirs for the taking. They'd fold me
in their formal motion, rhymed with sea and light,
self-possessed, not really interested in me.
To evaporate in that traffic air
with them, delivered to some place
I never knew before. I made it to
the other end. Next week I'll try again.

Some Voice

Past the silky gondola hulls
arcaded in the boatyard,
we walked that afternoon
to our favorite grubby campo,
empty except for cats
and one plane tree, with bench.
We loved it so much. We walked
just to be there, imagining
sometime we'd spend the night.
The little hotel, its frank lantern,
its dim sign dimmer by day,
we'd remember, just like that.

The tree's patchy shades worked
down your arm as it pointed up,
over there, locating the voice,
its open window, the soprano scales
tipped down to us. All life
is hidden life. Don't believe
everything you hear. To us,
or not to us, her voice fell
into that year, then ten more.

Routine practice doesn't call
to anyone, it simply falls
through footbridges, black hulls,
and plane tree. When we went back,
the singing wasn't there for us.
We take what's given and work
with that. The rest is grace.

UFO

Remember the desert's bluish light?
Dawn or late day? We drove long hours
to clarify our love with speedy talk,
road games we rehearsed but didn't play.
The two-lane blacktop swelled toward us
through sage and rabbitbrush, while we picked
at recent jealousies, glittery ghosts of fact,
whom you or I would sleep with, whose lips we liked best.

You slept on it. Evening, it must have been.
I kept driving on pills and coffee.
Curled loosely in your seat, you breathed
as you still do, hissing softly,
worn out by lost checkbook or keys.
I imagined someone else's touch on your thigh,
then touched it without waking you.
The stars began to shine outside the windshield.

That's when I saw the round flat lights,
five of them, like star points.
Bright invisible lines locked them in place
until they moved, switched hemispheres,
here, there, hummingbird style.
I pursued them, trying to catch up
while I shook your leg so you could watch
with me. They waited only until you woke.

You believed what I said, I think,
not in what I'd seen. They were there,

they were not. They saw me
with the same eye with which I saw them.
What I met there, while you slept,
is exactly what I've just said again to you.

Driving to Provincetown

"So where *is* Poussin in America anyway?"
    "There it is. That's him."
Our windows runny with parkway foliage
    while a road crew pours tarmac
across the meridian, black roller aghast
    with summer's steaming workers
vapored in half sun, their mock orange vests
    like the weepy sunset starting
behind the slickered yellow cab. The pharaoh
    sent them to construct
this high road to the sea. Not knowing
    any other way or world,
they pause a moment at the forge of their work
    while the dump truck chutes asphalt
before the roller that rolls on all alike.
    Some are waving their arms,
or red flags or stop signs, doubled
    in the dust of Egypt's desire.

The Bull-Roarers

Young men in an Australian tribe are seized by masked men, carried far from their familiar surroundings, laid on the ground, and covered with branches. For the first time they face an absolute darkness made terrifying by the approach of divinity announced by the bull-roarers.
                                        —Mircea Eliade

They come for me when it gets dark.
Large and silent, wearing mummers' masks,
badger claws chinging at their waists,
orange street cones on their heads
like party hats, tied with gut.
They lift and carry me from bed
to a field by our red movie house,
to bury me in a pit they've primed.
The stars rub their great noise on me.
I think: *I have my own things to bury
before it gets too late.* Herewith, first,
I bury anger, may its sparky pus
not touch my lips again hardly ever.

Second, into the pit I send greed,
may it choke on its hairy tongue.
Go down, you too, covetousness,
and lick the earth's dungy scabs.
But for myself I keep the following:
Lust, my favorite panic. Charity
for my friends and a few exceptions.
Desire, because what else is there
when warm chestnuts split their skins?

Last, I keep willfulness,
to shoot my mouth off as I please,
even when the roaring buries me
and dirt crawls ear to throat to tongue.

Hermes: Port Authority: His Song

Hey, mister, find your bus for you?
I burn my tracks, I stink,
I lay down in the dust.
Pardon me, I meant lie. Make time.
Try restrooms, bathrooms, toilets.
Read *Time*, the *Voice*, or *Times*.
Nobody believes the subway bombs,
landlords planting land mines
in tunnels where I live
and lay me down to sleep at night.
Show you to your bus
or an excellent candy bar?
A dollar's good. A quarter, too.
Any bus will do.
We got them all. There's Teaneck,
the Oranges and Hackensack,
Atlantic City, too,
those gonads and gourmets,
Robert Goulet and Eydie Gormé.
I'll sell you pussy, nookie,
what you will. I'll soap
your goodies in the men's room sink.
O play me how you will.
Sleep tight. God speed your bus.
A dollar, quarter, dime will do.

Girl with Pearl Earring by Johannes Vermeer

He put the spirit essence
the light pip not only
in each eye's albumen
concentrate of starlight
but must have been taught
how to do that by first
finding it in the pearl
he posed then corrected
in dusty studio light
that pounced on the window
behind which sits the cheeky girl
pear- and apple-blossom cheeks
a fake description naturally
of their plain fleshiness
drably golden and her lips
from Haight Street's darlings
nose studs jacket studs
girls with that kind of eye
one by the ATM machine
casual juicy and so fair
a Netherlandish type
panhandling strangers
pomegranate seed ball
bearings agleam in her nose
pearls not sea-harvested
but imagined seen put there
by a certain need and fancy
because love says it's so
picture that picture this.

Stanzas

At the Cole and Carl dog-run park,
mutts and poodles sniff grass,
couples laugh, the N-Judah
sharks from its tunnel. I'm druggy
while my doctor fools with dosages
to stagger my soul's bad chemistry.

I need a looser world and words for it.
Last night I watched the Dog Star burn
blue then frosted mercury. *Late Show*
station break, I write lines like these,
looking for exacter, plainer poetry
while more stars appear. I hate mornings—

my bed's a mudlake writing pulls me from.
Poetry's muscled homemade demon
sits on me and asks: "What next?"
A mockingbird sings from its nest,
dark or light the same, singing
end to end, while the kitchen light

curls me over short, easy books,
dumped crosswords, and *Vanity Fair.*
Then life's casual rush stops,
everywhere I look
the lymph in things goes dead,
though the world still shines the same.

Medicated to this willowed balance,
I don't weep now to see dogs run

or wild fennel bend to winds
kiting a tern from its brilliant marsh.
I don't get sick with fright to hear
an eyelash click across the street.

Little lab-rat gods rattling
in my jar, keep me close enough
to smell dog fur and fresh-cut grass.
Take away whatever you want,
but deliver me to derangements
of sweet, ordered, derelict words.

Add Salt

Prometheus lighted a torch at the sun and broke from it a
glowing coal which he thrust into a fennel stalk.

The AMERICAN GNOSTIC CHURCH marquee
fizzes in my window's broken capillaries
caused, the conductor says, by new glass
reacting to the air. I feel fogged in.

Here again are pied scrapmetal cubes
and racked junkers freaked by light,
and here I am again trying to say
what I see. It makes me hungrier.

The horse track's floating island,
the English Language Institute,
car wash, tar-shingle roofs,
U-rent lockers, and taprooms.

Same commute, same things in their orders
briefing past my view. Still looking
for the invisible life of things,
I can't get beyond or into amassings

and breaks of matter, green clabber
scumming puddles alongside the train,
then brickyards banked on body shops,
homeless trackside nappers under trees,

ditchwater where shopping carts come to drink,
where wild fennel thrives, as in Sicily,
to receive yellow embers our hero stole
to crown the graygreen stalk.

Its lacy tops I'll toss with macaroni
and fresh sardines from Monterey—
licorice feathers, movie houses, anisette
women served men on holy days,

                                   Pernod, too,
white like my window, or a Sazerac
greened with absinthe, O how it bends
yes to wind wash and bayshore gusts.
Next stop I'll step off and pick a bunch,

boil a pot of water in the aisle,
blow the sullen coals alive,
and invite the regulars and pony players,
my place at eight, we can talk over dinner.

(for August Kleinzahler)

Police

How oddly quiet
the squad car's light rack
flashing late tonight,
double-parked on my street,
the sea-chilled dark
tweaked by blues and reds,
the old sleepy houses
gap-toothed and aroused
like jack-o'-lanterns,
moments before you phoned
to say the doctors found,
sooner than expected,
new hot spots, metastasized
in her femur, vertebrae,
lung, and brain, making
of course no noise,
your voice how calmly
familiar with whatever's
worse and imaginable
repeating what you said
just weeks ago about
"the geometrical rigor
of retributive forces
in the universe"
while the car throws
its important lights
against the uneventful night.

Duboce Park

Late March and warmer drafts
kicking barefoot children at their kite strings

on grassy onion-dome shadows.
Purple gables, street lamps,

coy finials and stick facades
legislate the scene.

Kite strings drooping S or U,
our weather and daily measure

of blue sky, sea breeze,
slippages in the atmosphere,

children who reach to a heaven
beyond the buckling lines,

not quite on our ground,
gusting from us while

squinty nannies make crowns
of wisdom braids built of grass.

Higher up, cooler invisible lines
appear to us who think we see,

where kites don't catch the wind
and flesh-haunted emptiness

sketches us to ourselves,
bony, crosshatched, dreamy

for deity or dreaming it,
a heaven that falls and fits

this earth, these house rows, backyards,
the dog paths worn into the grass,

the sandbox and its twisting swings
empty where the children were just now

before they ran behind the kites,
running from us and our feeble facts,

as if another god shouts in their hearts,
scrambled, messier, but loving those

who run through soft grass, looking up
to Bat Signal or dragon bandoneón.

Brother Fire

(2004)

Brother Francis to Brother Leone

In my dream I watched it
from a windowsill *Come see this*
raptor's shadow hushed
down green-brick tenements
Bulk beak and feather struck
and tumbled aslant the air
with sparrow or chimney swift
Wilderness breathes wherever
we are and headed to O'Hare
late fall I saw on its vague
bare branch a goshawk
grace yes and auspicious terror
I should watch with him
I should be poorer than
any wing of the air

If you could have seen
(this is a different story)
above us cloud studies
out of Constable
Pescadero's sandstone cliffs
steeped and chewed by tides
I held Brother Antonio's hand
so afraid was he the cliff
would crumble *What was that?*
as if what then came had
already happened the osprey's

sea-foam breast
sign we said of the Holy Spirit

pounding the wind
Lift and save us it stormed
up beneath our feet
Alone in Inverness
I saw a kestral stop
in the blue and stoop
and icy blowtorch points
pecked my hands and feet
blood frothed from my side

Closer now my minders
watch and bear with me
while I'm walking barefoot
through a Tucson suburb
mesquite and prickly pear
a young peregrine
surveils me from the eye
of midmorning's sun
Last night Easter Saturday
I saw a deer enter
a bare-chested Yaqui ancient
who obeyed the dance
danced through him the poor
we think aren't with us
everywhere the deer-dancer's
concrete ramada beside the freeway
and reservation projects

Brother Ash
the less I become of what

God made me the more real
I am in His heart
Let durable goods be ashes
to pour on our heads
Brother Wing
keep me in my place
on lower Market Street
with that bare-chested man
bird of beautiful want
speechifying clothed
in chaps rat-food blanket
and cherry running shoes
Lady Poverty at his side

I walked Avenue A
Knee-deep in crows spirits
of murderers and suicides
croaking *Whatever's given*
I'll take away
Drenched in a Jersey storm
I tried to send my spirit
to God my core my sphere
I asked the hawk *Who are you?*
but in some nameless place
doubled-up overcoats pushed
oxcarts past me through mud
and hungry gray children
ate their cardboard name tags
Keep and bless such images
of our own killing kind?

Buzzards slice the silence
over our heads waiting
for us their food song
How little it takes to complete
a world to find what suffices
To Brother Fire I offer
our endless poor-men's wars
our starved ruined planet
song of thrush and whitethroat
beaks of meaningless fire
piercing our hands and feet
and offer wealth to Brother Ash
and waste of blood to Brother Rag.

All in One Day

Fat crows chop from leafless elms
and sail like shadows across my window,
nervous souls backlit by a reddish sky
full of snow that hasn't fallen yet.
Waxwings passed last month
to stuff their crops with holly berries.
Starlings cry from wires . . .

    Today's news says
a dark, unworldly matter makes up
the universe we call ours, passing through
everything, leaving no trace, we're drenched
with energy that blows stars apart
and farther from us speeds explosions
I see in dreams, like last night, when
each time I named a constellation
it became another.

    On a day like this,
crows budding on the crabby oaks,
the blood ghosts I see in human forms
could be a necessary fantasy
of nerve cells, dopamine, or appetite,
bodies modeled from phantom fluids,
passing through a world that doesn't exist,
or exists in the mind of God.

    I thought the child
hooting at a ruff of fallen leaves
would shovel them at me like a war
or bridal game, but the armfuls scooped
above her head rattled down,
wrinkled flames on her shoulders,

and she tested its atomized perfume,
clapping her orange mittens, fall's
first child, hollering
  Come down here, you!
That's when I felt most alive
inside matter's reechy stuff,
unseen, intensely real.
Later, riding into town,
held and rocked by the L's steelworks,
from my seat I saw the season crouch
behind the platform, and a college girl,
pigeon-toed and pale,
  standing there
in bawling November, rails and gravel
moonlit like snow, the world's freaked bark
scraped to pith, an express blowing through
whipped leaves around her feet . . .
Our mud-flake life, and rain sheets,
contracting to a brown, glassy drop
that clung to her reddening hair.

Dancing on New Year's Eve at Dave and Sheila's

"Everybody's looking for something"
and everything smells good.
My sweating partner's hips
push harder into mine,
tequila yeasting through our skin
and we'd lick each other dry,
drink more, do it again
while blue lamps twitch
between the others lost,
until someone at midnight
kills the music, calls us
to the front door where we grab
and kiss whoever's near,
squeezed out into the night
where wooly pops like corks
or muffled distant gunshots
are gunshots in fact, high times,
bullets to the stars.
They won't fall to earth here
where in June mysterious
citron lilies bloom, a perfume
more intense than lemons.
How did they get here?
Eyewitness News tells us
what guns cost there, beyond
the freeway. We smell ourselves,
the grand cedar by the door,
peanuts, booze, and sweat.
How can we not love them?
When the music snaps on again,

we weave back to the floor
adrift in each other's arms,
and love it more, that constancy
of beat and song,
she presses her mouth
to my ear, rubs harder with me
and sings We're here because
we're here because we're here.

The View from Here

It's not hard to find them any night, sleeping under autumn stars,
the nameless, swept away or under, asleep or dozy, car heater off,
a gentle poisoned wind blowing through the window, the toddler
kicks and growls like a dog dreaming, the older son's closed eyes
twitch as if he can't chase or flee those pictures fast enough,
and the parents, too big and hot, how every hour or so they wake,
touch, nudge to make room in their early model front seat,
fresh water to last the night, chips and Snickers, diapers, gum,
celebrity gossip rags, cover sheets for the children,
breathing inside sullen steel blued by moonlight, under a trestle
or interstate, in an off-season stadium lot, untended campground
or back street, or parked there behind a strip mall's Dumpster pod,
just like last night, times before and to come, if we look to see,
then to imagine all the tribes, junkers amassed like tortoises,
in an abandoned drive-in, windows steamy, voices and grunts
as we walk past the secrets of day jobbers, housecleaners,
nannies, pickers, and busboys camouflaged among us, on their way
to greater goods, dreaming of how we stand here watching them.

The Girl Found in the Woods

She planned it to perfection,
studied to fall a certain way,
the correct distance tree limb
to ground, as if in consciousness
she rehearsed the completed scene
she'd live into, a string of pictures
in her suburban remoteness,
the drop measured and tested
like any nuance of despair,
a cool day pressured by head winds
she bent her body through,
biking miles from town to scout
this place nobody would find,
to the liveoak she hangs from
observed by lesser birch and gum,
while her natural self told friends
she needed time *(Whatever you do,*
don't worry) alone, to ride the hills
she loved. And so she disappeared
into whatever sound her heart
flushed through her head, certain to spare
others the shame of finding her.
In that silence, after she stepped
or jumped, or slipped, from the bough
that creaked from the sudden flight
of weight, the clearing ticked
with ground squirrel, coyote, deer,
who walked past pictures training
across their eyes. Rock, bush,
tree branch, mistletoe.

Increased Security

Venus, demure tonight, as always, sharp
in my western sky which flops each time
the Fourth of July's sheet-lightning fireworks
blow from the eastern side of town, hooping
embarcadero lights, black bay and bridge,
star light, star bright, seer, solid and chaste
in her infinitude, calmly waiting
to watch the oceans buckle, cities burn,
while Catherine wheels and maypole pom-poms mock
her constancy, far-off sugared surprises
flaring orderly reds and purpled blues
above the silent pod of black-and-whites
and fireboats, fighter jets cruising,
chopper beams fingering the crowd
I can't see here, don't need to see to know
that while kids sing a jingling brass band march,
be kind to your web-footed friends
for a duck may be somebody's mother,
the sky shrieks at Venus, mother of all,
who watches from her distance, hears booms
and alarmed whistles over the heads of mothers
who squeeze their children's hands, fathers boosting
sons and daughters up onto their shoulders,
the better for them to catch the air, for balance,
still grabbing at the artificial fires
we all look up to, while we wait for more.

"How Do I Get There?"

Make the first left
then follow your headlights
chasing all those leaves
out West River Drive
full of increase late
fall maples and oaks
drive past Boathouse Row
the Schuylkill on your right
past the dead power station
and greatly gilt Joan of Arc
riding Franklin Parkway
to liberate the museum
so don't forget to salute
Rubens and the rest
ignoring riverside lights
spooled inside the water
and shrunken freeway ramps
night traffic creases
bear right at City Hall
more leaves newspapers
butterflies in taillights
then take Broad Street south
go until it's all
brickfronts and corner stores
right again on Wolf
watch for the wilder kids
playing after dark
check your mirrors lock
your doors now everything listens
for you while you pass

Baldini's Funeral Home
where more than ever the air's
a gasp of running leaves
that crackle under your tires
so follow them until
they grab the marbled steps
and then you'll know you're there.

(for J. T. Barbarese)

Didn't You Say Desire Is

like the elephant fog
shredded north
a white sun going down
Bessemers fired
through clouds horizoned
on my dog-eared stack
It feels good and right
to waste earnest hours
of an early evening's
daylight saving time
in uncertainty and want
these cranky climates
changing in us while we
haven't started dinner yet.

Sometime Nights

Sweetest meat
close to the bone

commonplaces
things known

pronouncements
come be my love

take it or leave it
get here you

old facts
flesh rags

the morning fog's
shorn whitecaps

I touch your
damp hair spooned

on the pillow
salt and meat

we two negatives
on window panes

How you sway
in our burly air

your slow way
tights first

bra blouse skirt
pinned-up hair

bracelet rings
full-size mirror

check everything
make sure you're there.

Blue Moon

(OCTOBER 31, 2001)

They're gathering now
Coneheads ghouls Spider Man
fly-by-nighters' burnt-cork cheeks
flailed sheets and twiggy voices
Mama stalking a border dog's
crescent around back around
as if to fend off certain harm
October's second sodium moon
basting the street and barbecue ribs
and links she smoked all day
to keep her four boys close
no begging door to door not
with new monsters wakened
Anything can happen here
tonight unlike past years free
to knock and shriek
now they spook themselves
overdub hip-hop shouts going
nowhere fast these fearless fat
boys past whom skip fuzzy whelps
tittering mice and bunnies clamped
to adults who keel them house
to house and now I see them
as a broken flock of dispersed
wild children wandering
adults and myself among them

like medieval gangs of the blind
the destitute the deranged the lost
beyond our ranks of city lights
to beg and thumb our way
suburb to rail tracks to hills
across lunar stubble fields.

A Man of Indeterminate Age on Subway Grate

The city loves inside my head

    In the morning fever all through the night

The city lives inside my head

    I got steam heat I got

Do not remove this person

    I am of the Holy Spirit see us rise

I am the police I am loving

    Inside garment trucks my ears brains what have you

Who feels what I hear in my mouth

    Running shoes pumps wing tips sandals stilettos

I think I have a bone in my stomach

    Here hey how did I get here

I'm the body of the city and immense with subways

    And if you should survive to one hundred and five

Floating up here that howl down there is me

       Of our time invisible angel

Of castoffs replays tax frauds lost lease sales

       Roaring steel wings hover above to take us

Cigarette holder

       It wigs me

Ortlieb's Uptown Taproom

The sax's rayon shirt tonight fires up
flamingos, pink parrots, blue palms . . .
He trues his porkpie so the pinky diamond
winks into the smoky room. The drummer
looks beyond us all, seeing things
we don't, winged things cutting the air.
A second set at midnight, the brewery long
closed down beyond that door. After their shift,
the cookers and machinists passed through
for beers and shots, punched Bobby Darin
into the jukebox. By 3 a.m. they're home,
leftovers in the oven, or TV dinners,
upstairs a sea of restless candied dreaming
(roller skating on ice, a red wet finger
in the toaster) and when he sits to eat,
he remembers waking as a child
to mountain bagpipers in his village,
Christmas morning, peasant music wheezing
high and thin down under the window.
Their goatskin bags call like animals,
the herdsmen's arms muscled like his own
checking heat and pressure gauges,
breathing a tune dreamed up as he goes along,
like our flamingo sax, in his ecstasy tonight,
who blows bagpipe music through our hearts
and the sudsy breath of drinkers quitting work.

Prayer Meeting

Hankies and sheets, hopeless routine longing,
my mother and I in the cellar twice each week,
her Sunbeam coasting under screws of steam,
me on my knees by the ironing board
to call Hail Marys. Our bodies vapored
into immaculate words. Shirttails talked back.
I wanted more than what I prayed for.
Her music-box antiphons mumbled us
around the decades. Neither of us knew
why or what we implored. God jerked alive
in repetitions. I reeled Him in. She must
have been appeasing me because she feared
offending Him, deity of hurt and rue,
of affliction and splintered rafters weeping
wan work dungarees, school uniforms,
all together in our separate voices.
The God of iron, unsatisfied, hissed back.

10 P.M. in Kezar's

The arrangement's vague at first.
Pocket doors half-open,
young hands at a piano,
vinyl-covered sofa, lamp
lighted by a sunny window,
each shifting as if uncertain
of its place, until a woman
filling out a fruity apron
beside me—*Here, big boy*—
offers a quarter-moon
of fennel bulb.
I bite, the scene goes still,
a salty fleshiness
in my mouth.
        Now,
the woman in the apron,
the child and her étude,
and so many others gone,
something vapors in
this free brandy the barkeep
sets out, a new product,
have a taste, but I'm
about to weep for loss
over these anise hints,
so to appease myself
I offer it back to her,
who sniffs, shakes her head,
and says it must be me.

Honey

We four were fat with talk
under their fresh-painted pergola.
You giggled sounds like *blue spruce*
and *hollyhocks*, he told us how
he chicken-wired dirt chaos
into that terraced garden,
she announced road-stand watermelon
while the smart scout did its work.

Yellow jackets write such precise
expectations on the air.
You dummied up when one,
sensing sweet melon flesh,
alighted to sample nectar
on your lips. I watched it
wanting more, wanting in
to probe your tongue,

and you watched me as if I were
someone or somewhere else.
The day before, for no reason,
"Death that hath suck't the honey
of her breath" looped in my ear,
and now came again
while we waited for the sting, or cry,
that didn't come.

Romeo's words played back
like children's nonsense rhymes,
when this morning's storm drained

212

yellow jackets to my ligustrum tree,
its spermy scent plied with sweet broom
and lemon blossoms like those in their garden,
when the wooer petted your mouth
and you smiled as if you knew
it couldn't hurt, your eye on me,
making sure we understood
you make your charms available
but don't give them away.

The Kiss

The mossy transom light, odors of cabbage
and ancient papers, while Father Feeney
polishes an apple on his tunic.
I tell him I want the life priests have,
not how the night sky's millions
of departing stars, erased by city lights,
terrify me toward God. That some nights
I sleepwalk, curl inside the tub,
and bang awake from a dream of walking through
a night where candle beams crisscross
the sky, a movie premiere somewhere.
Where am I, Father, when I visit a life
inside or outside the one I'm in?
In our wronged world I see things
accidentally good: fishy shadows thrown
by walnut leaves, summer hammerheads
whomping fireplugs, fall air that tastes
like spring water, oranges, and iron.

"What are you running from, my dear,
at morning Mass five times a week?"
He comes around the desk, its failing flowers
and Iwo Jima inkwell, holding his breviary,
its Latin mysteries a patterned noise
like blades on ice, a small-voiced poetry
or sorcery. Beautiful dreamer,
how I love you. When he leans down,
his hands rough with chalk dust
rasp my ears. "You don't have the call,"
kissing my cheek. "Find something else."

On the subway home I found
a Golgotha air of piss and smoke,
sleepy workers, Cuban missiles drooping
in their evening papers, and black people
hosed down by cops or stretched by dogs.
What was I running from? Deity flashed
on the razor a boy beside me wagged,
it stroked the hair of the nurse who waked
to kiss her rosary. I believed the wall's
filthy cracks, coming into focus
when we stopped, held stories I'd find
and tell. What are you running from,
child of what I've become?
Tell what you know now
of dreadful freshness and want,
our stunned world peopled
by shadows solidly flesh,
a silted fountain of prayer
rising in our throat.

A Cold June

Ice, dirt, gray miraculous flesh. I can put my finger on the space debris
burred all night on my window, until fog effaces it and other signs.
What am I looking for? This comet dust that seems to burn recalls
the cold basilica, in June, my pious friend and I invited to the altar,
the priest (sour voice, sour heart) reciting: locked in the reliquary, livid,
translucent, like a flake of trapped ash, floats a slice of Christ's heart,
it's all true, doctors testified, what looks like a dragonfly's wing
is His living blood cells. How curtly he announced it, impatient
with non-belief before it showed itself, impatient with my indifference,
while my friend wheezed through his mouth, awed, worshipful,
and the father looked from him to me, as if to say you can't love
without astonishment, the miraculous wants innocence beyond knowledge
of contradiction, not the monocle of my unbelief. Yet now each night
the comet somehow cuts across the relic, a coincidence I can credit
because it makes no sense, to believe in what I know is not true life.
The stars and gods have made us so that we make meaning of what
resists us, and of such resistance make a consciousness, a rotund
coherence of accident and law. The imagination in one stroke
squeegees subway passages, manhole-cover steam cones, clouds,
bus wheels' blowback snow, the dance of minor things
sifting from or into others, momentously. I smudge an afterimage
on my window to mark a juicy slice of being. What happens now?
Buses and cafés explode in holy lands, in Hackensack
a father kisses his son in peace, money eats dirt on Wall Street,
Big Casino overdoses across the street, the Gypsy to the Werewolf sings
Even a man who is pure at heart and says his prayers by night
Will become a wolf when the wolfbane blooms, and the moon is full and bright.
Glacial dust wasting away across the sky where gods have come and gone,
downstairs a student's cello practices praise and questions for those gods.
Woeful, nervous, almost content, he falters and plays the phrase again.

New Poems

_____

Them Again

I don't have to call them,
I never know when they'll buzz,
the pests, then they can't
stop talking, like taxi static
on the phone behind
whatever living voice
I'm trying to hear.
And now they're back.
A headset twitters
near the famed Korean
who rides our bus repeating
"Remember me, remember
me to everybody"
that streams into wingbeats
when blackbirds slap trees
then pretend to leave. I never know
where they'll be, my skittish
talky dead, in dozens sung
by girls skipping rope,
Mama told Papa don't be so bad,
or deer bounding down court,
Get back, pick him up!
They talk their talk
and claim me: my father
who hardly spoke at all;
a brain-fevered friend
cussing Jesus in tall cotton;
another who lived to quarrel
and still can't shut up,
like fanatical mosquitoes,

ladybugs clogging the screen,
or gossipy mob of moths
stuck to the underside
of our incomplete existence,
batting their opaque wings
at our brief blackbird world,
so much noise and so it goes
when this big-nosed redhead,
before getting on,
sucks and dumps his smoke,
jet-trailing through the door—
he hacks and he hawks
and he sets them loose again
to crowd me, saying the same
senseless things they say.

Night-Lights: Providence Amtrak Station

On the platform, sick with myself
for reasons I hardly recall,
—in the tunnel's whippy trash
the oncoming locomotive lights
looked intimate and frothed—
I thought (of course) I'd jump,
to see what I could see.

But my angle reversed itself,
and I remembered instead
driving the Schuylkill Freeway
past 30th Street Station, looking in
at shed, silvered rail yards,
mousy lights, switching tracks
like tracer lights arcing forth
all directions to some other where,
when I considered the thousands,
the loved and the estranged I never knew,
emerging from the underworld,
unhappy, unfree, but on the move.

On that dark, low-ceilinged platform,
I knew, or convinced myself I knew,
that if I fell into those cataract lights
and stopped, the way we fall
in dreams until we stop,
I might see God's face because
I'd see all things at once.

What held me back
was your image, earlier that night,
pointing to a full moon briared
in a beech's circled branches.
There it would be, once a month,
unconscious and available,
alive, as we're alive and here,
in stark, lovely, godless repetitions
good or bad, sustaining us, as is:
circle, light, branch, recurrence
to hold us in our place in time.

The Wedding Dance

Indigo sequins trash
the circle's center,
and she knows that,
dancing there,
she'll outlive everyone.
Women jitterbugged.
Men clutched sweaty
Seven-and-Sevens.
Roast beef sandwiches,
cream soda, red-eyed heirs
skating sawdust boards,
somewhere a bride and groom.

At our table, my father
("Let's break this up")
grabs my arm and gimps
toward the dancers' circle
and its untouchable one,
where he light-foots
snappy fat-man moves,
happy storybook dragon,
boilermakers on his breath,
sexed up, cutting the boards,
while itchy at the edge
I blur into forgetfulness.

We're never really free.
Because he's not dancing,
but stops at the sizzling edge,

watches, bums his bad leg
back to our desolate table.
What pity if not born to live
in a world you're born to?
Rim shots knock for us who are
too far to see her turn
and laugh inside the circle,
her alluring moves for us
and anyone who dares.

Overlooking Lake Champlain

Rain spills leaf to leaf, rips some down
the chilly greenblack air, falls and falls
until it tamps October's ripened ground
that sponges up big plans. Sheet lightning
popped across the water and rubbed things raw.
The rain's tinny cymbal-brushing rushes
our nerves—we'll live how long to hear it?
Eighty today, Gracey on the back porch rocker
tells her daughter tidy, sewed-up thoughts
of killing extremities, what things they saw:
chairs, rugs, sheep, dogs, one cow,
bobbing in the torrent that November,
nineteen sixty-six, the Arno running
so swift it caught your breath, how she and child
slogged alongside ancient Florentines
(books, cabinets, pots) saving what they could.

Our rain gives in to dull, fuzzy sun
while Fran details her plans, next month,
to go back, first time since the flood, insists
she weirdly remembers what wasn't yet there
to be seen: plaques and carved waterlines
that mark church and palazzo and cut time
in place. Thoughtless excess runs through things,
death floods our nature before it even comes.
"You were this high" (pointing at the lake)
"the water was *here*." Like a priestess, palms lifted
as if to gather and elevate us, the air, the instant,
wet leaves dropping while the rocker creaks
and she nods to nap in the expanding sun.

1864

Like true believers elated by what they've seen,
as if at the end of days, raptured away
like millions more of undying credence,
this Union soldier's ankles crossed,
his ditch-mate's demure arms folded
like an Annunciation angel's,
others flank to flank, mouths catching flies—
how candid and unharmed they look,
these teens in O'Sullivan's snapshot,
grimy mother-of-pearl faces
aspiring to another life or way or time,
who see where we don't. Who among us can say
(we the quick, fattened, fed, sheltered,
alive because we look and grieve)
what they saw, what stiff promise
their brains made or erased,
or what millions today on TV will see
in empty combat boots spread on a lawn,
far from their desert, clownish and collapsed
for lack of feet they never fit quite right?

The Little Flowers

My neighborhood's newest dreamboat
taking his morning coffee. Flip-flops,
pajama top, hair screwy from bed—
girls in cupcake pigtails notice
the coy, coltish looks,
but off his meds the atmosphere
clogs up, he says, with goofy dust.
Joy or jaybird panic crushing
his skull, head cocked
at birds not flying past,
smiling up, heaven sunbathing,
loosing love to purplish ethers
in his head, now maypoling
the parking meter a million children
and me in shorts and Keds
round-dancing with him,
then back to mug and book,
tipsy rock-a-bye in his chair,
big head aswish, singing a little
Happy to be loved by you.
Dear stranger, keep it light,
Jim Dandy to the Rescue
or frivolous *fioretti* hymn
to your air of birds not there,
to irrelevant brick and sky,
to the Pacific so close still
not close enough to hear.

Buddy Caesar and His Starlighters

Everything's going up in smoke.
Lake Island's oaks hug mid-
summer's chemical sunset,
a slow rusty Philadelphia burn
burring dusty treetops, first stars
coming on, and the neighborhood
turns out, kings and queens
in beach chairs, other unfurred
creatures on blankets, or in trees,
all eyes on the hopping crowd
before the bandstand, hard-
pedaling "In the Mood" then "Cherokee."
Buddy cues slurpy trombones
and even the fatter no-no's rise
and shuffle to the dancing ground,
old-style jitterbugs spiking dirt
at century's end. I'm off to the side,
taking things in, I've learned to do that,
to watch, to smile at the fire, but now
this flutter-tongue solo breaks me down,
dust spanks sandals, mules, and sneaks,
stars divot whiter in the blacker blue,
time feels round and I'm in it,
with twilight's jumpy Dago sounds,
awake now, swinging with a stranger.

The Fruits of the Sea

First time we've met, her ex–lover boy and I, seated together,
both of them long settled in other beds. She's in the kitchen:
thin hands, bumpy knucklebones of the dancer she once was,
picking over halibut chunks, squid, mussel flesh,
whatever she fancies, crab meat last. In Barnegat,
my first time out, the traps rattled with blue crabs
hooking the cage, clawing themselves—the sea rang
like her pots and pans and heirloom silverware.

I knew the story he didn't tell, about their young affair.
Unfinished images: heavy-muscled braid to her waist, leggy,
toe shoes pegging their marks, finding in that body in the mirror
the desired line. On the water, I knew the sun pressing my back
would smart. She later said that while the Love God and I jawed,
the new wife dropped by the kitchen. "I came to greet the help.
I like your new head"—razor-cut to salt-and-pepper cap.
"We want to seem our age but never really look it, right?"

I see her in her prime, before the injury, soaking rehearsal tights,
tulle, or Daisy Mae jeans, steaming windows to nail a combination.
"He was the world's weirdest lover, never let me see him naked.
I wonder how Wonder Girl handles that." She's stirring rice now.
Muscles seam her forearm; a lifted shoulder tugs the apron string
tighter to her neck. "He had to be first in bed, before I came in,

an undercover man, room totally dark." The crabs
are in the kitchen in their traps, any motion she made died
in the moment it danced through, we're famished, here because
we want more of more, and now she's bringing the goods.

(for Karen Wilkin)

To Aphrodite

Lady Know-It-All
bittersweet
apple incense
incensing my room
cigarette smoke
in the ceiling fan
my Kewpie doll
assassin sister to
that virus Ares
who can't be trusted
and like you kills
everything in sight
O old friend
hologram skin
wrinkles and all
adrift from some
disturbed place
with trouble in mind
be with me now
big of promise
and give me what you got.

Two Pain Poems

1. "I Can't Tell You What the Pain Is Like."

Who fed me steel filings I didn't taste going down?
   And these deposits in marrow and blood?
   Plant your foot. It clanks, spikes to the ball joint.
A fleshy fire burns in the cellar of the spine,
   a matter of faith, believe it, carve it out,
   take the florid lump outside and fucking bury it.
Hershey Park's Barrel o' Fun's hardwood wall,
   the body stuck, then ripped loose, raw skin strip
   that worms and weeps to an unreachable center.
Dream on, O mopey dopey, of women singing in the kitchen,
   wet mattress dirt sucking your coccyx,
   you're not going anywhere, starfish.
That summer concert on the lawn, J. Strauss mit bier und pretzels,
   poor armadillo, try to get back on your feet,
   set your back upright, your tipsy gravestone.
Not your body, yours all the same, kiln-fired in the not you,
   so of course it keeps you awake, yours
   to do with, and what did you expect?

2. "A Blue and Mighty Expanse"

Hallway voices from a kitchen in another house
inside mine—I'm muscling out of sleep—
tra-las dubbed over anatomies, clothes, hair
of no specific aunt or tasty salesgirl,
a beckoning vibraphone in my rib cage.

I should get closer, face their faces: light
cuts their silhouettes, they stretch their necks
to get on pitch and sing to me. My call remains
the same: Wait for me, don't stop, heal these bones
broken by the bloody coral I've slept on.

Their room rafts deeper into the sea-swell house,
my bed wails from the shore, their *hallow hollow*
floats into gristled air, my mattress sprouts green
steel wires that bind my legs and spine and truss me
into waking when I watch their voices go.

The Green Man

rumdumb from last night's shrubbery tryst
exhales soot, fernseed, shoots and vines,
brings his hot breath from the city park's wood,
saying a song we don't understand
through the briar and bay leaves of his beard.
And in Philadelphia, 1954,
out of late autumn's darkening he came,
a junkman tugging a Penn Fruit cart,
straw bristling his face, crying a name.
Or from manholes in other cities,
his holographic ectoplasm greets us
when traffic lights turn green.
Uncover and there he is, membranous
Caliban alone with sewers rats,
or stumblebum Puck, unnameable solids
crusting nails and toes, bringing us his dark.
Or our neighborhood's soused John-John,
cobra down-at-heel boots skidding
at my feet among the maddening jasmine,
when I grab too late to save him growls:
"I can save you darling pigs.
Behold, behold, and maybe I'll help."

Solo R&B Vocal Underground

It seems to head from its last stop too fast,
my transbay train's strung-out *hoo*, deep
inside the tunnel, and starts to bleed
into the baritone wail of that guy
at platform's end, a sort of lullaby
rubbed against the wall then caught in a squall
of wind darkening toward us, his whippy voice
skinning its tired song off the tiled dome:
he's determined, the silky lyric says,
to be independently blue, while we all
wait to be chuted to car lot or home,
closer to love, or farther, and sooner to loss,
our bashful shoes and arms like lives crossed,
every plural presence now some thing alone,
thanks to our singer-man. We wait for the train,
patient with hope, a hope that's like complaint.

Cab Ride Downtown

And salted was our food
in snowy April, a long board
and friends in Spanish Harlem,
shot glasses, skirts slapping knees,
and my old-style artist friend
snakes his arm to the bouzouki,
then skates his hand
across butcher paper
and sweeps you into form
right there: "Just a thing,
you know? A nothing drawing."
The belly dancer's working
a little too hard and thereby
shows inferior artistry,
and for her next act
knocks a waiter's tray
that splashes you, I mean
the picture Paolo made,
with burger grease. Only a few
curved and straight lines
—like hill and horizon—
the nature of you,
your fairness and light,
we all said, gestured just so
into life, and you said
Look at these stains,
three times said it,
remember? Instructing yourself
in disbelief, inside our cab,
snow still falling,

April holding on,
you holding the ragged page
you'd restore overnight
with sufficient salt,
so when you said
Ah, well, nothing's perfect,
there were things
still left to say.

Chicago and December

Trying to find my roost
one lidded, late afternoon,
the consolation of color
worked up like neediness,
like craving chocolate,
I'm at Art Institute favorites:
Velázquez's *Servant*,
her bashful attention fixed
to place things just right,
Beckmann's *Self-Portrait*,
whose fishy fingers seem
never to do a day's work,
the great stone lions outside
monumentally pissed
by jumbo wreaths and ribbons
municipal good cheer
yoked around their heads.
Mealy mist. Furred air.
I walk north across
the river, Christmas lights
crushed on skyscraper glass,
bling stringing Michigan Ave.,
sunlight's last-gasp sighing
through the artless fog.
Vague fatigued promise hangs
in the low darkened sky
when bunched scrawny starlings
rattle up from trees,
switchback and snag
like tossed rags dressing

the bare wintering branches,
black-on-black shining,
and I'm in a moment
more like a fore-moment:
from the sidewalk, watching them
poised without purpose,
I feel lifted inside the common
hazards and orders of things
when from their stillness,
the formal, aimless, not-waiting birds
erupt again, clap, elated weather-
making wing-clouds changing,
smithereened back and forth,
now already gone to follow
the river's running course.

City Dog

On my viral fingertips,
in my feverish veins,
the city remembers
everything on the run:
the sidewalks' bad nerves,
ashy air like old comic books,
the unchanged changeful
powders and cement dust
from far construction sites,
and windborne wetness
strumming in my stomach.
Everything's present.
Fog French-kisses
steam from manholes,
a rottweiller pines
for the sexy sheltie runt
dumbstruck by a banana peel.
I'm unrisen, stale, still alive.

———————

Too early in the morning
for "Radar Love"
raging from a low-rider.
It's bad enough these smells
on the streetcar corner
rake my head and confuse
peppercorn perfume, coffee breath,
coconuts in some brunette's hair—
the pied veil between me

and whatever's next
when right now I want all
the little that can be had.

———————

If the dead could speak
(Savinio says)
we would hear them
from their distant prison
crying every night:
Don't leave us alone
Don't leave us alone.
Through the dark outside
a barroom mirror's bottles
spin like roulette slots
across windows shot
by acetylene sparks.
The city ghosts itself.
Don't leave us alone.

———————

Disco Rollerbladers in the park
(line-dancing Frankenstein Rockettes),
wheelbarrow strollers,
weepy eucalyptus shedding medicinals,
the fuschia and the foxglove
and ragtag lovers on the grass,

in a city only, if you please,
for the country will give us no peace,
nor save or heal us.

————————

Our streetcar gypsy,
baubles, bangles, and beads,
counts out his sad singles;
I'll take his saloon sourness,
sleepy after-school girls life-
jacketed in parkas, pet cockatoos,
dead shoes, earrings, earbuds,
someone's boombox whining:
Love on a Saturday night
When the world's lights
Get low and we get high.
The animal of song,
its sweet diminishings,
passed singer to singer,
all of us more wakeful now,
choral moans and whispers
ebbing through the crowd . . .

NOTES

"Lucky Lucy's Daily Dream Book" (page 26): The dream books once (perhaps still) sold at newsstands in South Philadelphia, derived from the ancient Neapolitan dream book called a *smorfia*, alphabetically listed dream subjects along with an explanation of their meaning and a corresponding number that determined which three-digit bet to place with the local bookie.

"Second Horn" (page 55) refers to a painting by Carpaccio of St. George slaying the dragon, hanging in a small chapel-like room in Venice.

"Emmaus" (page 93) owes something to Caravaggio's treatments of the subject.

"The Restorers" (page 101): The poem's epigraph is taken from Jacopo de Voragine's hagiography, *The Golden Legend*. The walls of the Strozzi Chapel in Florence narrate episodes in the life of St. Philip and are notable for the wiggly mannerist frescoes by Filippino Lippi, who had worked with Masaccio in creating a fresco cycle in the Brancacci Chapel that features the often reproduced *Expulsion of Adam and Eve*. Masaccio's *Trinity* hangs near the Strozzi frescoes in Florence's Santa Maria Novella.

"The Sicilian Vespers" (page 109): In Verdi's opera set in thirteenth-century French-controlled Palermo, the heroine, Hélène, after many complications, is united with her lover, Henri, a "good" Frenchman. At their wedding, the Sicilians revolt and rout the French troops.

"Frankie's Birthday Party" (page 121): Death Box is a Philadelphia street game in which players move bottle-caps through a series of numbered squares while avoiding the large central "death box," where a player must wait several turns before moving again.

"The Mummers" (page 151): Philadelphia's annual Mummers parade on January 1 dates to 1901 and features three "divisions": string bands, fancy brigades, comics. "The comic clubs continue to raise controversy over themes they use in the parade that make fun of current issues and news stories such as issues involving religion, ethnicity, and feminism. Many Mummers parade controversies over policies, such as the exclusion of women and the use of black-face, lasted many years." From www.mummers.com. In 1985, after a twenty-four-hour siege and gunfights, Mayor W. Wilson Goode ordered the police to drop a bomb on the West Philadelphia headquarters of a militant group called MOVE. Sixty other houses were destroyed.

"Ovid in Exile" (page 155) was occasioned by David R. Slavitt's translation, *Ovid's Poetry of Exile*, and its language picks up some of the spirit of that work.

"The Apples" (page 165): "Of the golden fruit which the earth gave to Juno at her marriage, [Hesiod] tells us of the Dragon:—'He, in the secret places of the desert land, kept the all-golden apples in his great knots.' We hear from other scattered syllables of tradition, that this dragon was sleepless, and that he was able to take various tones of human voice." John Ruskin, *Modern Painters*.

ACKNOWLEDGMENTS

The poems from *The Dog Star* are reprinted with the permission of the University of Massachusetts Press. The poems from *The Restorers* are published with the permission of the University of Chicago Press (© the University of Chicago. All rights reserved). The poems from *Shadows Burning* are reprinted with permission of Northwestern University Press.

The following poems from *New Poems* first appeared in periodicals: "Them Again," "Cab Ride Downtown," "Night-Lights: Providence Amtrak Station" *(The Harvard Divinity Bulletin)*; "The Wedding Dance" *(Threepenny Review)*; "The Little Flowers," part 1 of "Two Pain Poems," "1864," "Buddy Caesar and His Starlighters," "Chicago and December," "Solo R&B Vocal Underground," "City Dog," "The Green Man" *(Poetry)*; "Overlooking Lake Champlain" *(Ploughshares)*; "To Aphrodite" *(A Public Space)*; "The Fruits of the Sea" *(The New Criterion)*.

A NOTE ABOUT THE AUTHOR

W. S. Di Piero was born in South Philadelphia in 1945. He is the author of eight previous books of poetry, as well as three volumes of translation from the Italian. He writes about art for the *San Diego Reader* and has published four collections of essays and criticism on art, literature, and personal experience. His honors include a Guggenheim Fellowship, a National Endowment for the Arts grant, and a Lila Wallace–Reader's Digest Writers' Award. He lives in San Francisco.

A NOTE ON THE TYPE

The text of this book was set in a typeface called Bell. The original punches for this face were cut in 1788 by the engraver Richard Austin for the typefoundry of John Bell (1745–1831), the most outstanding typographer of his day. They are the earliest English "modern" type design, and show the influence of French copperplate engraving and the work of the Fournier and Didot families. However, the Bell face has a distinct identity of its own, and might also be classified as a delicate and refined rendering of Scotch Roman.

Composed by Creative Graphics, Allentown, Pennsylvania

Printed and bound by R. R. Donnelley, Harrisonburg, Virginia

Book Design by Robert C. Olsson

Printed in the United States
by Baker & Taylor Publisher Services